■SCHOLASTIC

Grades 3–5

Getting Started With the Traits

Writing Lessons, Activities, Scoring Guides, and More for Successfully Launching Trait-Based Instruction in Your Classroom

**Ruth Culham and
Raymond Coutu**

New York • Toronto • London • Auckland • Sydney
Mexico City • New Delhi • Hong Kong • Buenos Aires

Teaching
Resources

To all those intermediate teachers who have been there for us from the start and every day thereafter, particularly Mike Freborg, Pat McCarty, and Debbie Stewart. Our deepest thanks for your considerable contributions to our work.

Editor: Raymond Coutu
Production Editor: Sarah Glasscock
Cover design by Brian LaRossa
Interior design by Holly Grundon
Copy editor: Eileen Judge
ISBN-13: 978-0-545-11190-4
ISBN-10: 0-545-11190-0

Scholastic Inc. grants teachers permission to photocopy the reproducible pages from this book for classroom use. No other part of this publication may be reproduced in whole or in part, or stored in a retrieval system, or transmitted in any form or by any means, electronic, mechanical, photocopying, or otherwise, without written permission of the publisher. For information regarding permission, write to Scholastic Inc., 557 Broadway, New York NY 10012.

Copyright © 2009 by Ruth Culham

All rights reserved. Published by Scholastic Inc.
Printed in the U.S.A.
           4 5 6 7 8 9 10   40   15 14 13 12 11

Contents

Introduction 7

**Chapter 1: What Are the Traits and
What Makes Them So Great?** 9

The Traits and the Intermediate Writer 10

A Word on the Writing Process 14

- Lesson: Understanding the Writing Process 16
- Great Picture Books for Teaching About the Writing Process 17

A Word on Writing Conferences 19

- Talking to Students About Revision 19
- Talking to Students About Editing 20

Chapter 2: Assessing Student Work 22

Guidelines for Assessing Student Work 22

Scoring Guides and Scored Sample Papers 23

Scoring Guides for Each Trait

- Ideas 24
- Organization 25
- Voice 26
- Word Choice 27
- Sentence Fluency 28
- Conventions 29

Scored Sample Papers

- Paper #1, Grade 3 30
- Paper #2, Grade 3 31
- Paper #3, Grade 3 32
- Paper #4, Grade 4 33
- Paper #5, Grade 4 34
- Paper #6, Grade 4 35
- Paper #7, Grade 5 36
- Paper #8, Grade 5 37
- Paper #9, Grade 5 38

Chapter 3: Trait-Based Lessons for the Whole Class

Chapter 3: Trait-Based Lessons
for the Whole Class 40

Guidelines for Conducting Lessons 40

Ideas Lessons 41

   • Lesson #1: Finding a Topic 42

   • Lesson #2: Focusing the Topic 45

   • Lesson #3: Developing the Topic 46

   • Lesson #4: Using Details 47

Organization Lessons 48

   • Lesson #1: Creating the Lead 49

   • Lesson #2: Using Sequence Words 50

   • Lesson #3: Structuring the Body 52

   • Lesson #4: Ending With a Sense of Resolution 53

Voice Lessons 54

   • Lesson #1: Establishing a Tone 55

   • Lesson #2: Conveying the Purpose 56

   • Lesson #3: Creating a Connection to the Audience 57

   • Lesson #4: Taking Risks to Create Voice 59

Word Choice Lessons 61

   • Lesson #1: Applying Strong Verbs 61

   • Lesson #2: Selecting Striking Words and Phrases 63

   • Lesson #3: Using Specific and Accurate Words 65

   • Lesson #4: Choosing Words That Deepen Meaning 66

Sentence Fluency Lessons 67

   • Lesson #1: Capturing Smooth and Rhythmic Flow 68

   • Lesson #2: Crafting Well-Built Sentences 69

   • Lesson #3: Varying Sentence Patterns 70

   • Lesson #4: Breaking the "Rules" to Create Fluency 74

Conventions Lessons 76

   • Lesson #1 78

   • Lesson #2 79

   • Lesson #3 80

   • Lesson #4 81

   • Lesson #5 82

   • Answer Key 83

Publishing Tips 85

Chapter 4: Trait-Based Activities for Independent and Small-Group Work

Chapter 4: Trait-Based Activities for Independent and Small-Group Work 86

Ideas Activities

- Finding a Topic 86
- Focusing the Topic 87
- Developing the Topic 88
- Using Details 88

Organization Activities

- Creating the Lead 89
- Using Sequence Words 90
- Structuring the Body 90
- Ending With a Sense of Resolution 91

Voice Activities

- Establishing a Tone 93
- Conveying the Purpose 93
- Creating a Connection to the Audience 94
- Taking Risks to Create Voice 95

Word Choice Activities

- Applying Strong Verbs 95
- Selecting Striking Words and Phrases 96
- Using Specific and Accurate Words 97
- Choosing Words That Deepen Meaning 98

Sentence Fluency Activities

- Capturing Smooth and Rhythmic Flow 99
- Crafting Well-Built Sentences 99
- Varying Sentence Patterns 100
- Breaking the "Rules" to Create Fluency 101

Conventions Activities

- Checking Spelling 102
- Punctuating Effectively 102
- Capitalizing Correctly 103
- Applying Grammar and Usage 103

Chapter 5: Answers to the Questions Intermediate Teachers Ask Most 105

Are the traits a writing curriculum? 105

In what order should I cover the traits? 105

Isn't it punitive to give a score of 1? 106

Doesn't a score of 6 send a message that
there's absolutely no room for improvement? 106

How often should I use prompts to help students get started? 106

How should I teach spelling? 106

Why do parents worry so much about conventions? 106

Professional Resources Cited 107

Children's Literature Cited 107

Appendix

Revision Checklist 108

Editor's Marks 109

Student-Friendly Scoring Guides for Each Trait 110

Introduction

For years, we have been researching, writing about, and speaking about the traits of writing and their application at the intermediate level. In that time, we have learned that student writers benefit greatly from understanding how strong pieces of writing are created and how to apply that knowledge to their own work. Their growth soars, and watching that growth is quite remarkable. From coast to coast, the traits have found their rightful place in the writing classroom. We are always on the lookout for new ways to make the traits visible and help students use them as they learn to write. The work is evolving, becoming more nuanced and precise, as it should.

One of the most significant areas of development has been using the language of the traits as a basis for communicating with students about how their writing is progressing. Rather than opting for generic comments, such as "Good work!" and "Awkward," teachers are using the scoring guides on pages 24–29 as sources of specific comments to help students see where their writing is strong and where it could use revision and editing.

This book contains all the nuts-and-bolts information and materials you need to get started with the traits and begin achieving the success that so many teachers are already experiencing.

❈ Chapter 1 spells out what the traits are and are not, and their benefits. Each trait is clearly defined, with special considerations for weaving it into the intermediate classroom.

❈ Chapter 2 shows you how to assess papers for each trait and provide constructive feedback. You'll find reproducible scoring guides, step-by-step instructions for using those guides, scored sample student papers, and sample conference comments to help you hit the ground running.

❈ Chapter 3 contains 24 lessons organized around the key qualities of each trait so that you can get students to apply those qualities right from the start of the year. We also offer handy tips for teaching about the trait and annotated lists of picture books to use as mentor texts.

❈ Chapter 4 offers trait-based writing activities that students can do in small groups, in pairs, or on their own. These are teacher-tested activities, guaranteed to fire up students and get them to produce their best work possible.

❈ Chapter 5 provides answers to the questions teachers ask us most, such as "Are the traits a writing curriculum?" "In what order should I cover the traits?" and "How often should I use prompts to help students get started?"

We round out the book with an appendix that contains reproducible student-friendly scoring guides, a revision checklist, and an editor's marks chart to help you boost students' writing skills.

As you'll see in the appendix, the student-friendly scoring guides range from "Just Starting" at the lowest point to "I've Got It!" at the highest. Most likely, you're just starting your work in the traits. That's an exciting place to be. Let's go!

Chapter 1

What Are the Traits and What Makes Them So Great?

In this age of standardized tests, educational accountability, and "no fail" programs coming your way all the time, teaching writing in today's upper-elementary school is more difficult than ever. But it can also be invigorating, if you know exactly how to help students become the best writers they can be. That requires a focused approach. And that's the concept behind the traits of writing model—an effective, research-based tool for assessing and teaching writing.

You might be tempted to think the trait model is the magic box with all the answers inside. But no box is big enough for all the answers. And you know what? You don't need one. What you do need is a model for assessing and teaching writing that honors your wisdom and strengths as a professional.

That said, the trait model is more than an approach to assessing and teaching writing. It's a vocabulary teachers use with each other and with their students to describe what good writing looks like. Whether it's a story about a dancing cat, an essay on recycling, or a persuasive piece on the benefits of school uniforms, six characteristics make the writing work:

- ❀ **Ideas:** The content of the piece; its central message and the details that support it.

- ❀ **Organization:** The internal structure of the piece—the thread of logic, the pattern of meaning.

- ❀ **Voice:** The tone of the piece—the personal stamp of the writer, which is achieved through a strong understanding of purpose and audience.

- ❀ **Word Choice:** The specific vocabulary the writer uses to convey meaning and enlighten the reader.

- ❀ **Sentence Fluency:** The way words and phrases flow through the piece. It is the auditory trait and is, therefore, "read" with the ear as much as the eye.

- ❀ **Conventions:** The mechanical correctness of the piece. Correct use of conventions guides the reader through the text easily.

Chapter 1: What Are the Traits and What Makes Them So Great?

9

Once you know these traits and begin teaching with them, you will see them stand out in the work of your students. Your students will embrace the traits and become self-assessors with the skills to revise and edit their own work.

The trait scoring guides on pages 24–29 allow you to assess student writing and provide feedback that students can use to make their current and future work stronger. Scores range from 1 to 6 in each of the traits. For example, if a student writes the roughest of drafts, showing little control and skill in the trait for which you are assessing, he or she would receive a score of 1, "rudimentary." But if his or her piece shows strong control and skill in the trait, he or she would receive a score of 6, "exceptional."

Once you've assessed the papers, you can use the scores to determine the most appropriate targets for instruction. For example, if many of the students in the class score a 1 or 2 in organization, you would plan to teach and reinforce key qualities of this trait in lessons and activities over the next few weeks. Teaching to areas of greatest need: that's how we use assessment data as the focus for instruction.

This book brings the writing traits model to life by providing all the assessment tools, focus lessons, and extension activities you need to get started. The model is exciting, and it really works. And in today's world, effective models like the traits have never been more important.

The Traits and the Intermediate Writer

When students take the giant leap from learning to read to reading to learn, it's cause for celebration because they're using their skills to comprehend text and gain knowledge. The same is true for writing. When students move from learning to write to writing to learn, they're using their skills to *create* text and *share* knowledge. This leap typically happens during third grade, but we've found that it can happen as early as second grade and as late as fifth, depending on where a child falls on the developmental spectrum. As an intermediate teacher, you know that even though your students are approximately the same age, they don't possess the same skills—in writing or in any other subject. At the start of each year, you expect students who can write full-blown essays, students who can barely muster a paragraph, and students who can do everything in between.

Take a look at the two samples on page 11 written by third graders. The first writer is ready for the materials and ideas in this book, and the second for those in its companion book, *Getting Started With the Traits: K–2* (2009).

Sample 1

Do you like your house? I do, my house is my favorite place. Now your'e probably thinking this person is weird. You are wrong, if you thought about it a while you would think so to. Let me tell you about it. If you where alone how would you feel, sad, lonlely, something of the type. You see, the house contains the family, the food you eat and a shelter to sleep in. Can you live without these things? You can, for a while. But if you didn't have a family, you'd be lonely, if you had no food you'd be weak and hungry. If you had no shelter you would get colder and colder. A house contains things that make life better. I hope you keep these things in mind. For if you don't you will have to learn agian. This is one reason my house is my favorite place. Another reason my house is my favorite place, is makes me think of love. Love is very powerful, love is what connects everybody together. You are full of love. To live you have to love. to love you have to have a family and a family lives in a house. A house is a very important thing, remember this for ever. Remember that a house is very, very important. Just please remember that.

Sample 2

this is abut my dog Tippy. evey monning I go to her and Say I love her. win I wasa baby Tippy wuade lay by me and I love her very much.

For students to grow as writers, it's important to take them from where they are and move them forward one step at a time. After all, true differentiation means supporting students using methods that match their specific abilities and needs. You can determine the level of your students by assessing their writing using the scoring guides on pages 24–29. If a student's writing score is low, it's important to check it against the primary scoring guides (which you'll find in *Getting Started With the Traits: K–2*) to pinpoint what the student requires to get on track. All students have a right to know how to improve their work, regardless of how much they know about writing when they enter your classroom. Selecting the appropriate scoring guide is essential to making the traits work for you and your students. And fear not: the students you worry about most will make great strides in writing, as proven by students in writing-traits classrooms across the country and throughout the world.

Just look at these samples from a fifth grader. The first piece was written at the beginning of the year. The second piece was written after he had learned and applied the writing traits. What a difference time and the traits can make!

Sample 1

My Special Day!

On Summer I went to the beach I went with my family and I saw my friends I went with them in the water and we went to the sand an then we walked to rocks an we went fishing and I almost got a fish but it slipped of an then the fish went back to the water and then I went to the water to get a crab and the crab almost bit me sow I let it go back to the water an then I went to eat food an that was the best day ever.

Sample 2

Shopping with mom

Long ago when I was five or younger, while my mom was shopping, I would tag along. I always start dying of bordome. I could literally feel my body shutting down, my arms feel like noodles, my eyes drop down and my mouth refuses to swallow. But just then I would start thinking the entire store is a science fiction alien base. The employees would be armed, hostile aliens. Remember those little red coupon despensers. Well those would be auto-fire lazer cannons. And worst of all, the Forklift of DOOM! It was practically the mother alien all you had to do was run, and every time it makes a little beep noise that would mean it saw you and is going to hunt you, and you could not be seen by the employees, coupon despensers, and most of all, the forklift! Annnnd if I got bored of that, I would just keep on nagging my mom, "When are gonna get out of here!?"

Once you assess your students' writing, examine the results to determine which trait or traits require the most attention. Share results with students in conferences and conversations so they understand what they are doing well and what they aren't. Their interest will increase when they understand that the skills you are teaching are the same ones they need to become better writers. There's no point in keeping the secret to good writing a secret! (For more on assessing student work, see Chapter 2.)

In our experience, most intermediate students want to write. They take pride in their work. It's not unusual for us to be greeted in the morning by a student waving a paper and asking, "I wrote this last night. Will you read it?" Of course, we want to honor the request, and we usually do when writing time rolls around. We capitalize on the student's energy by reading the paper quickly, picking one trait or more, and conferring with him or her. Later, we might assess the paper more closely using the scoring guides to provide richer feedback, if we feel it will be useful to the writer.

Furthermore, we've found that most intermediate students not only want to write, they want to write long, complex pieces in a variety of genres and formats. As they hone their skills in those genres and formats that may be new to them, they learn that the writing world is a big place. So we must respond clearly, deeply, and precisely to their work, using the language of the traits to help them find their way. For example, we must teach them

> ## QUESTIONS TO CONSIDER WHEN GETTING STARTED
>
> Consider these three questions as you begin working with your intermediate writers:
>
> ❉ Am I using the developmentally appropriate scoring guide to assess my students' writing?
>
> ❉ Do the results show what students know as well as what they don't know?
>
> ❉ Do the results help me provide targeted instruction so each student continues to improve in measurable ways?

that writing well means more than choosing the first word that comes to mind; it means choosing the best words to make their message clear and compelling. And, we must teach them that real writers create more than stories or simple explanations; they create a wide variety of texts for specific purposes. In short, we must teach students the writing skills they need to write well, skills they will use the rest of their lives every time they write.

Intermediate students are eager, enthusiastic, and energetic. They've mastered the basics, and that feels good. It's important to keep in mind, however, that it hasn't been long since they knew very little about writing. Just a year ago, your students may have been struggling to get a simple sentence down on paper. Although their writing skills are gelling, they are not fully set. So be gentle. Demanding too much too fast will deflate them as surely as a pinhole will deflate a beach ball. Criticizing them will not motivate them. It will only discourage them. However, offering honest feedback, based on key qualities of the traits, deepens students' understanding of writing and lifts their confidence.

When you use assessment to guide instruction, you can plan and carry out your teaching more effectively and, as a result, see huge growth in your intermediate students' writing performance.

A Word on the Writing Process

The writing process is just that, a process. Its beginning, middle, and end flow like a river, always going somewhere but often taking its own sweet time to get there. The writing process enables us to show intermediate students what it's like to be a writer. It allows us to open the door to possibilities in writing, giving students topic choices, teaching them skills, showing them how to work through problems, and allowing them time to arrive at solutions. With it, we can demonstrate how to think aloud on paper and follow the steps that successful writers follow so students can do the same in their own work—and to remind them that these steps are flexible and recursive, not rigid and linear. In its most general form, the writing process looks like this:

Prewriting:	The writer comes up with ideas for the work.
	Predominant trait: ideas
Drafting:	The writer gets the ideas down in rough form.
	Predominant traits: ideas, organization
Sharing:	The writer gets feedback on the draft from a reader or listener.
	Predominant traits: ideas, organization, voice, word choice, sentence fluency
Revising:	The writer reflects on the draft and makes changes based on the first five traits.
	Predominant traits: ideas, organization, voice, word choice, and sentence fluency
Editing:	The writer "cleans up" the piece, checking for correct capitalization, punctuation, spelling, paragraphing, grammar, and usage.
	Predominant trait: conventions
Publishing:	The writer goes public with the finished piece.

Intermediate classrooms should be places where there are writing demonstrations and discussions every day about what comes next and why. They should be places where there's a strong connection between reading and writing, as students look to mentor texts as models. They should be places where teachers and students interact using trait-specific language to question if the work is clear and focused, if it is organized so the reader can see where the idea is going, if the voice is truly the writer's, if the words are accurate and precise, if the sentences flow smoothly, and, of course, if conventions are used correctly.

IS YOUR CLASSROOM PROCESS-CENTERED OR PRODUCT-CENTERED?

In a process-centered classroom:	In a product-centered classroom:
❖ Students work on different tasks at different rates.	❖ Students do the same tasks at the same rate.
❖ Teachers encourage many short, interesting pieces of writing, any of which may lead to one or two longer pieces over time.	❖ All students complete the same predetermined writing assignments.
❖ Students work alone, in pairs, small groups, and as a class.	❖ Students usually work alone.
❖ Writing is shared as it is being created.	❖ Writing is shared only when it's finished.
❖ One piece may lead to another on a new topic that is discovered during the writing.	❖ When a piece is finished, students ask for or are given the next task.
❖ Mistakes provide opportunities to stretch and grow.	❖ Mistakes are to be avoided. Emphasis is placed on getting it right the first time.
❖ Questions like these are typical: *Does this work? What else could I try? Will you help me find a better way to say this? What would happen if I changed it to show . . . ?*	❖ Questions like these are typical: *Is this long enough? Is this what you want? Is this going to be graded?*

Every time our intermediate writers put pencil to paper, they should realize that they have choices—that the writing process is a series of flexible steps for them to use to help them write well. In the next section, we present a lesson to help you build that understanding.

Chapter 1: What Are the Traits and What Makes Them So Great?

15

UNDERSTANDING THE WRITING PROCESS

I n this lesson, students learn, from the author's perspective, how ideas germinate into full-blown stories. *What Do Authors Do?* (1995), the book upon which the lesson is based, shows clearly where ideas come from, how they are drafted and revised, and how they wind up as books. It's a charming book, intended to teach and entertain at the same time.

MATERIALS:

❋ a copy of *What Do Authors Do?* by Eileen Christelow

❋ cut-apart list described in step #1 below

❋ pencils, pens, markers, crayons

❋ drawing paper

WHAT TO DO:

1. Make an overhead transparency of the following list, cut apart the items, and mix them up.

   ❋ Think of an idea using a favorite book or a memorable experience as inspiration. Talk about it with another writer before you write.

   ❋ Write your idea down and add details.

   ❋ Read your draft to another writer. Does he or she have suggestions to make it better?

   ❋ Keep writing. Add pictures.

   ❋ Check the writing for mistakes. Compose a final copy.

   ❋ Share your finished piece with family members and friends.

   ❋ Start planning your next piece.

2. Read *What Do Authors Do?* showing the pictures as you go.

3. Tell students they are going to capture the steps of the writing process that Christelow describes in her book.

4. Pick up a transparency strip, read it aloud, and ask students to help you decide where this step goes in the writing process. Move each strip to make room for the new one, changing the order as necessary.

5. When you have all the strips in order, read them aloud with the students. Ask if there are other steps in the writing process that they recall from the book and, if so, where these steps fit into the list.

6. Make a bulletin board showing each item in the list. Group students in pairs and ask them to illustrate one of the steps. Place their creations next to the appropriate items on the bulletin board to help students remember the steps.

FOLLOW-UP ACTIVITIES:

❖ Ask students which step of the writing process they feel will be the easiest for them and which will be the most challenging. Discuss ways that writers overcome difficulties.

❖ Read and discuss *Ish* (2004) by Peter H. Reynolds. Talk to students about how every writer feels "ishy" about what they write, but over time, with lots of help, this feeling turns to confidence.

GREAT PICTURE BOOKS FOR TEACHING ABOUT THE WRITING PROCESS

Aunt Isabel Tells a Good One
Kate Duke, Author and Illustrator
Dutton, 1992

This adorable book explains how writers work with character, plot, and setting to tell stories. Penelope, a young mouse, and her Aunt Isabel work out all the elements of a clever story, including the use of details to capture the reader's interest. For example, Aunt Isabel adds villains as she explains to Penelope that stories must have problems to be resolved. This text is a terrific place to begin discussions of what makes a good story as students plan their own pieces.

Chapter 1: What Are the Traits and What Makes Them So Great?

17

You Have to Write

Janet S. Wong, Author

Teresa Flavin, Illustrator

Margaret K. McElderry, 2002

Stepping into the shoes of the student writer who is told to write but really doesn't want to, Wong shares valuable ideas about how to get going: the smallest everyday events or observations can make fascinating reading. An appreciation of the difficulty of learning to write winds through this book. Wong anticipates what will challenge students most and provides the inspiration to find the ideas that will excite those students as writers and, in turn, engage us as readers.

Author: A True Story

Helen Lester, Author and Illustrator

Houghton Mifflin, 1997

Lester's autobiography of her writing life is a treasure. She documents her first writing effort—a grocery shopping list only she could read—to her attempts at writing a picture book and getting it published. Throughout, the reader is reminded that writing is hard, that ideas come from everywhere, and that many runs at the text are necessary to get it just right. Lester's personal journey as a writer is a celebration. Though she is honest about the struggle, she is joyous about the outcome. Students who read this text will get a balanced view of the writing process.

Show, Don't Tell! Secrets of Writing

Josephine Nobisso, Author

Eva Montanari, Illustrator

Gingerbread House, 2004

One of the secrets to good fiction and nonfiction writing is to be descriptive and help the reader fall deeply into the idea. In this visually appealing and interactive book, Nobisso puts the just-right adjective with a noun to make the writing come to life. (Yes, you get to feel textures and push buttons for sounds.) She explores the use of metaphors and similes, too, helping the reader see how images can be created by using all the senses.

A Word on Writing Conferences

Whether they're completing an assignment that you give them, such as one of the activities in Chapter 4, or a self-initiated writing task, students benefit from conferences, in which they feel safe to air their accomplishments and struggles—and receive substantive, constructive, individualized feedback from you.

TALKING TO STUDENTS ABOUT REVISION

Always begin with something you notice the student can do, something that is working well, and then move on to what is yet to be learned. Don't start with criticism. For instance, you might notice that the piece contains very precise, sophisticated words. Compliment the writer; this is a huge deal. After that, you can point out something that needs attention, such as sentences that begin the same way, but again, don't start with criticism. In this all-important battle to help students see themselves as writers, we must take time to recognize the knowledge and skills they bring to the writing table. It's always easier to work on problems if you have already established that there are strengths.

In students' work, no matter how rough, look for early indicators of success. For example, the writer may be experimenting with time by alternating verb tenses or using the words *now* and *later*. Perhaps he or she has played with new words and sound patterns, or reinvented old ideas in new, quirky ways. These are entry points to support the revision process. Notice what students are trying to do and praise it. Celebrate small victories. Stretch their thinking; encourage them to be patient and keep at it. If you have questions, begin them with "I wonder." Tread carefully because the message we send to our younger writers can determine how willing they are to move their work forward and take ownership.

Also, when talking to students about their work, use *and*, not *but*, to connect the comments. *And* implies that writing is a continuous process and supports your positive statement; *but* negates it. For example, "I'm really into your description of the spaceship, Charles. Your details make your idea clear to me. And now, let's work on organizing those details for better flow."

See below for some simple questions students should ask themselves as they revise their work for ideas, organization, voice, word choice, and sentence fluency. Feel free to give students individual questions or clusters of questions, depending on their levels and needs, and revise the questions to be developmentally appropriate.

Ideas

❋ Does my writing make sense?

❋ Does my writing show that I understand my topic?

❋ Is my writing interesting?

Chapter 1: What Are the Traits and What Makes Them So Great?

19

Organization

❖ Do I start off strong?

❖ Are all my details in the best possible order?

❖ Are similar thoughts grouped together?

Voice

❖ Can the reader hear me in the writing?

❖ Can the reader tell I care about this idea?

❖ Is the voice I've chosen right for my audience?

Word Choice

❖ Do the words I've chosen sound and feel just right?

❖ Have I used words that I've never used before?

❖ Have I painted a picture with words?

Sentence Fluency

❖ Does my writing sound good when I read it aloud?

❖ Do my words and phrases flow together?

❖ Have I included sentences of varying lengths and with different beginnings?

TALKING TO STUDENTS ABOUT EDITING

Unlike revision, editing is about cleaning up the text to make it readable. When we assess intermediate writing for conventions, we look for skill in punctuation, capitalization, spelling, paragraphing, and grammar and usage. In other words, we look at whether the piece meets the conventions of writing.

The first step in teaching editing skills to intermediate students is to identify which skills they already have and which ones they don't by using the scoring guide on page 29. Otherwise you run the risk of giving students editing activities they don't need or that are too challenging for them. On page 21 are some questions to share with students to help them understand conventions. Post these under the heading "Editing Questions," clearly separating them from the revision questions listed in the last section.

Conventions

❋ Is the punctuation correct and does it guide the reader through the text?

❋ Did I capitalize all the right words?

❋ Is my spelling accurate—especially for words I read and write a lot?

❋ Did I follow grammar rules to make my writing clear and readable?

❋ Did I indent paragraphs in all the right places?

Concluding Thought

Plain and simple, the traits help students become better writers. The model empowers students to think like writers, talk like writers, and write like writers because it gives them the language to do so. The stunning simplicity of the traits, the shared vocabulary that they generate, will add energy—an "I can do it" spirit—to your writing program. It's a privilege for us to share the ideas in this book with you.

Chapter 1: What Are the Traits and What Makes Them So Great?

21

Chapter 2

Assessing Student Work

When students are presenting their ideas clearly on paper—when they choose a great topic and support it with important details, when they compose a strong sentence made up of carefully chosen words, when they try a new genre using the appropriate voice for that genre—they deserve to hear from us, their teachers, about what is working and why, and how proud we are of their accomplishment. Conversely, when students are struggling, they depend on us for clear, focused direction. Targeted, trait-specific feedback is what student writers need to progress.

That's why the kind of assessment we're about to describe is so important. It gives you the background knowledge you need to provide that targeted feedback, by asking you to delve deeply into the text to communicate what you discover to the writer. It's far more useful than traditional assessment based on rubrics that lead to a single score. You get precise, concrete information about your students as writers, and your students get truly constructive responses to their work. This chapter gives you both parts of that essential equation: what to look for and what to say.

Guidelines for Assessing Student Work

We won't lie. Assessing your first few papers may be challenging and time-consuming. It's important, though, to give it your best effort. If you invest energy in understanding the different performance levels for each trait now, it will pay off later. In fact, it will make your job easier, more effective, and more enjoyable. To get started, simply follow these guidelines.

1. Choose a paper that, upon a quick reading, shows strengths and/or weaknesses in particular traits that you wish the student to work on further.

2. Assess the paper using the scoring guides that appear on pages 24–29. Read the scoring guides' descriptors for each of the six levels, from top—6: *Exceptional*—to bottom—1: *Rudimentary*. Assign a score of 1, 2, 3, 4, 5, or 6 to each of the traits and write it on the paper or in your grade book.

3. Pinpoint specific items from the scoring guide on which you want to focus. Don't overwhelm the student by choosing too many items at once. Pick one or two items that capture the student's strengths and one or two that capture weaknesses, and leave the rest for another paper or another day. For example, maybe you want to focus on the child's stellar lead and the less-than-stellar spelling. Or maybe his or her use of vivid details or sophisticated words. Or maybe the voice—how natural it sounds . . . or doesn't.

4. As the student becomes more skilled, progressing past the *Rudimentary* and *Emerging* stages, think about making one comment about revision (ideas, organization, voice, word choice, or sentence fluency) and one about editing (conventions).

5. In your discussions with the student, begin with something he or she is doing well. Then gently move on to something the student should do next. For more advice on working with individual students, see pages 19–21.

Remember, your goal should be to collect data that captures what students do well so they can do it again, and what they're not doing well so you can help them do it better. It's not about the numbers or scores; it's about clear communication on writing performance. The better you know the scoring guides, the more skilled you'll be at assessing papers.

Scoring Guides and Scored Sample Papers

The nine sample papers on pages 30–38 capture the wide range of writing skills typically found in grades 3 to 5. Review the scoring guides on pages 24–29, read each paper closely, assess the paper, and then read our scores and comments to see how they compare to yours. Do the sample papers reflect the writing of students in your classroom? Try out the scoring guides on your students' work after you've practiced on these.

Keep in mind that, since intermediate writers benefit as much from oral communication as written, it's important to hone your skills at finding just-right words for use in conferences, small groups, and even whole-class lessons. So we've provided comments on each paper to serve as examples of what you might say.

Scoring Guide: Ideas

The content of the piece, its central message and the details that support it.

HIGH

score **6**

score **5**

Exceptional

A. **Finding a Topic:** The writer offers a clear, central theme or a simple, original storyline that is memorable.

B. **Focusing the Topic:** The writer narrows the theme or storyline to create a piece that is clear, tight, and manageable.

C. **Developing the Topic:** The writer provides enough critical evidence to support the theme and shows insight on the topic. Or he or she tells the story in a fresh way through an original, unpredictable plot.

D. **Using Details:** The writer offers credible, accurate details that create pictures in the reader's mind, from the beginning of the piece to the end. These details provide the reader with evidence of the writer's knowledge about and/or experience with the topic.

Strong

MIDDLE

score **4**

score **3**

Refining

A. **Finding a Topic**: The writer offers a recognizable but broad theme or storyline. He or she stays on topic, but in a predictable way.

B. **Focusing the Topic:** The writer needs to crystallize his or her topic around the central theme or storyline. He or she does not focus on a specific aspect of the topic.

C. **Developing the Topic:** The writer draws on personal knowledge and experience, but does not offer a unique perspective on the topic. He or she does not probe the topic deeply. Instead, the writer only gives the reader a glimpse at aspects of the topic.

D. **Using Details:** The writer offers details, but they do not always hit the mark because they are inaccurate or irrelevant. He or she does not create a picture in the reader's mind because key questions about the central theme or storyline have not been addressed.

Developing

LOW

score **2**

score **1**

Emerging

A. **Finding a Topic:** The writer has not settled on a topic and, therefore, may offer only a series of unfocused, repetitious, and/or random thoughts.

B. **Narrowing the Topic:** The writer has not narrowed his or her topic in a meaningful way. It's hard to tell what the writer thinks is important since he or she devotes equal importance to each piece of information.

C. **Developing the Topic:** The writer has created a piece that is so short the reader cannot fully understand or appreciate what the author wants to say. The writer may have simply restated an assigned topic or responded to a prompt, without devoting much thought or effort to it.

D. **Using Details:** The writer has clearly devoted little attention to details. The writing contains limited or completely inaccurate information. After reading the piece, the reader is left with many unanswered questions.

Rudimentary

Scoring Guide: Organization

The internal structure of the piece—the thread of logic, the pattern of meaning.

score 6

HIGH

Exceptional

A. **Creating the Lead:** The writer grabs the reader's attention from the start and leads him or her into the piece naturally. The writer entices the reader, providing a tantalizing glimpse of what is to come.

B. **Using Sequence Words and Transition Words:** The writer includes a variety of carefully selected sequence words (such as *first, second,* and *finally*) and transition words (such as *however, also,* and *clearly*), which are placed wisely to guide the reader through the piece by showing how ideas progress, relate, and/or diverge.

C. **Structuring the Body:** The writer creates a piece that is easy to follow by fitting details together logically. He or she slows down to spotlight important points or events, and speeds up when it's necessary to move the reader along.

D. **Ending With a Sense of Resolution:** The writer sums up his or her thinking in a natural, thoughtful, and convincing way. He or she anticipates and answers any lingering questions the reader may have, providing a strong sense of closure.

score 5

Strong

score 4

MIDDLE

Refining

A. **Creating the Lead:** The writer presents an introduction, although it may not be original or thought-provoking. Instead, it may be a simple restatement of the topic and, therefore, does not create a sense of anticipation about what is to come.

B. **Using Sequence Words and Transition Words:** The writer uses sequence words to show the logical order of details, but they feel obvious or canned. The use of transition words is spotty and rarely creates coherence.

C. **Structuring the Body:** The writer sequences events and important points logically, for the most part. However, the reader may wish to move a few things around to create a more sensible flow. The reader may also feel the urge to speed up or slow down for more satisfying pacing.

D. **Ending With a Sense of Resolution:** The writer ends the piece on a familiar note: "Thank you for reading," "Now you know all about . . . ," or "They lived happily ever after." He or she needs to tie up loose ends to leave the reader with a sense of satisfaction or closure.

score 3

Developing

score 2

LOW

Emerging

A. **Creating the Lead:** The writer does not give the reader any clue about what is to come. The opening point feels as if it were chosen randomly.

B. **Using Sequence Words and Transition Words:** The writer does not provide sequence and/or transition words between sections or provides words that are so confusing the reader is unable to sort out sections.

C. **Structuring the Body:** The writer does not show clearly what comes first, next, and last, making it difficult to understand how sections fit together. The writer slows down when he or she should speed up and speeds up when he or she should slow down.

D. **Ending With a Sense of Resolution:** The writer ends the piece with no conclusion at all— or nothing more than "The End" or something equally bland. There is no sense of resolution, no sense of completion.

score 1

Rudimentary

Scoring Guide: **Voice**

The tone of the piece—the personal stamp of the writer, which is achieved through a strong understanding of purpose and audience.

HIGH

Exceptional

A. Establishing a Tone: The writer cares about the topic, and it shows. The writing is expressive and compelling. The reader feels the writer's conviction, authority, and integrity.

B. Conveying the Purpose: The writer makes clear his or her reason for creating the piece. He or she offers a point of view that is appropriate for the mode (narrative, expository, or persuasive), which compels the reader to read on.

C. Creating a Connection to the Audience: The writer speaks in a way that makes the reader want to listen. He or she has considered what the reader needs to know and the best way to convey it by sharing his or her fascination, feelings, and opinions about the topic.

D. Taking Risks to Create Voice: The writer expresses ideas in new ways, which makes the piece interesting and original. The writing sounds like the writer because of his or her use of distinctive, just-right words and phrases.

Strong

MIDDLE

Refining

A. Establishing a Tone: The writer has established a tone that can be described as "pleasing" or "sincere," but not "passionate" or "compelling." He or she attempts to create a tone that hits the mark, but the overall result feels generic.

B. Conveying the Purpose: The writer has chosen a voice for the piece that is not completely clear. There are only a few moments when the reader understands where the writer is coming from and why he or she wrote the piece.

C. Creating a Connection to the Audience: The writer keeps the reader at a distance. The connection between reader and writer is tenuous because the writer reveals little about what is important or meaningful about the topic.

D. Taking Risks to Create Voice: The writer creates a few moments that catch the reader's attention, but only a few. The piece sounds like anyone could have written it. It lacks the energy, commitment, and conviction that would distinguish it from other pieces on the same topic.

Developing

LOW

Emerging

A. Establishing a Tone: The writer has produced a lifeless piece—one that is monotonous, mechanical, or repetitive, and off-putting to the reader.

B. Conveying the Purpose: The writer chose the topic for mysterious reasons. The piece may be filled with random thoughts, technical jargon, or inappropriate vocabulary, making it impossible to discern how the writer feels about the topic.

C. Creating a Connection to the Audience: The writer provides no evidence that he or she has considered what the reader might need to know to connect with the topic. Or there is an obvious mismatch between the tone and the intended audience.

D. Taking Risks to Create Voice: The writer creates no highs or lows. The piece is flat and lifeless, causing the reader to wonder why the author wrote it in the first place. The writer's voice does not pop out, even for a moment.

Rudimentary

Scoring Guide: Word Choice
The specific vocabulary the writer uses to convey meaning and enlighten the reader.

score 6

HIGH

score 5

Exceptional

A. **Applying Strong Verbs:** The writer uses many "action words," giving the piece punch and pizzazz. He or she has stretched to find lively verbs that add energy to the piece.

B. **Selecting Striking Words and Phrases:** The writer uses many finely honed words and phrases. His or her creative and effective use of literary techniques such as alliteration, simile, and metaphor make the piece a pleasure to read.

C. **Using Specific and Accurate Words:** The writer uses words with precision. He or she selects words the reader needs to fully understand the message. The writer chooses nouns, adjectives, adverbs, and so forth that create clarity and bring the topic to life.

D. **Choosing Words That Deepen Meaning:** The writer uses words to capture the reader's imagination and to enhance meaning. There is a deliberate attempt to choose the best word over the first word that comes to mind.

Strong

score 4

MIDDLE

score 3

Refining

A. **Applying Strong Verbs:** The writer uses the passive voice quite a bit and includes few "action words" to give the piece energy.

B. **Selecting Striking Words and Phrases:** The writer provides little evidence that he or she has stretched for the best words or phrases. He or she may have attempted literary techniques, but they are trite for the most part.

C. **Using Specific and Accurate Words:** The writer presents specific and accurate words, except for a few related to sophisticated and/or content-related topics. Technical or irrelevant jargon is off-putting to the reader. The words rarely capture the reader's imagination.

D. **Choosing Words That Deepen Meaning:** The writer fills the piece with unoriginal language rather than language that results from careful revision. The words communicate the basic idea, but they are ordinary and uninspired.

Developing

score 2

LOW

score 1

Emerging

A. **Applying Strong Verbs:** The writer makes no attempt at selecting verbs with energy. The passive voice dominates the piece.

B. **Selecting Striking Words and Phrases:** The writer uses words that are repetitive, vague, and/or unimaginative. Limited meaning comes through because the words are so lifeless.

C. **Using Specific and Accurate Words:** The writer misuses words, making it difficult to understand what he or she is conveying, or uses words that are so technical, inappropriate, or irrelevant that the average reader can hardly understand what is being said.

D. **Choosing Words That Deepen Meaning:** The writer uses many words and phrases that simply do not work. Little meaning comes through because the language is so imprecise and distracting.

Rudimentary

Scoring Guides

Sample Papers

Lessons

Activities

FAQs

Scoring Guide: **Sentence Fluency**

The way words and phrases flow through the piece. It is the auditory trait and is, therefore, "read" with the ear as much as the eye.

 score 6

HIGH

  score 5

Exceptional

A. **Capturing Smooth and Rhythmic Flow:** The writer thinks about how the sentences sound. He or she uses phrasing that is almost musical. If the piece were read aloud, it would be easy on the ear.

B. **Crafting Well-Built Sentences:** The writer carefully and creatively constructs sentences for maximum impact. Transition words such as *but, and,* and *so* are used successfully to join sentences and sentence parts.

C. **Varying Sentence Patterns:** The writer uses various types of sentences (simple, compound, and/or complex) to enhance the central theme or storyline. The piece is made up of an effective mix of long, complex sentences and short, simple ones.

D. **Breaking the "Rules" to Create Fluency:** The writer diverges from standard English to create interest and impact. For example, he or she may use a sentence fragment, such as "All alone in the forest" or a single word, such as "Bam!" to accent a particular moment or action. The writer might begin with informal words such as *well, and,* or *but* to create a conversational tone, or he or she might break rules intentionally to make dialogue sound authentic.

Strong

 score 4

MIDDLE

  score 3

Refining

A. **Capturing Smooth and Rhythmic Flow:** The writer has produced a text that is uneven. Many sentences read smoothly, while others are choppy or awkward.

B. **Crafting Well-Built Sentences:** The writer offers simple sentences that are sound but no long, complex sentences. He or she attempts to vary the beginnings and lengths of sentences.

C. **Varying Sentence Patterns:** The writer exhibits basic sentence sense and offers some sentence variety. He or she attempts to use different types of sentences, but in doing so creates an uneven flow rather than a smooth, seamless one.

D. **Breaking the "Rules" to Create Fluency:** The writer includes fragments, but they seem more accidental than intentional. He or she uses informal words, such as *well, and,* and *but,* inappropriately to start sentences, and pays little attention to making dialogue sound authentic.

Developing

 score 2

LOW

score 1

Emerging

A. **Capturing Smooth and Rhythmic Flow:** The writer has created a text that is a challenge to read aloud since the sentences are incomplete, choppy, stilted, rambling, and/or awkward.

B. **Crafting Well-Built Sentences:** The writer offers sentences, even simple ones, that are often flawed. Sentence beginnings are repetitive and uninspired.

C. **Varying Sentence Patterns:** The writer uses single, repetitive sentence pattern throughout or connects sentence parts with an endless string of transition words such as *and, but, or, because,* and so on, which distracts the reader.

D. **Breaking the "Rules" to Create Fluency:** The writer offers few or no simple, well-built sentences, making it impossible to determine if he or she has done anything out of the ordinary. Global revision is necessary before sentences can be revised for stylistic and creative purposes.

Rudimentary

Scoring Guide: Conventions

The mechanical correctness of the piece. Correct use of conventions (spelling, capitalization, punctuation, paragraphing, and grammar and usage) guides the reader through text easily.

score 6

HIGH

Exceptional

A. **Checking Spelling:** The writer spells sight words, high-frequency words, and less familiar words correctly. When he or she spells less familiar words incorrectly, those words are phonetically correct. Overall, the piece reveals control in spelling.

B. **Punctuating Effectively:** The writer handles basic punctuation skillfully. He or she understands how to use periods, commas, question marks, and exclamation points to enhance clarity and meaning. Paragraphs are indented in the right places. The piece is ready for a general audience.

C. **Capitalizing Correctly:** The writer uses capital letters consistently and accurately. A deep understanding of how to capitalize dialogue, abbreviations, proper names, and titles is evident.

D. **Applying Grammar and Usage:** The writer forms grammatically correct phrases and sentences. He or she shows care in applying the rules of standard English. The writer may break from those rules for stylistic reasons, but otherwise abides by them.

score 5

Strong

score 4

MIDDLE

Refining

A. **Checking Spelling:** The writer incorrectly spells a few high-frequency words and many unfamiliar words and/or sophisticated words.

B. **Punctuating Effectively:** The writer handles basic punctuation marks (such as end marks on sentences and commas in a series) well. However, he or she might have trouble with more complex punctuation marks (such as quotation marks, parentheses, dashes) and with paragraphing, especially on longer pieces.

C. **Capitalizing Correctly:** The writer capitalizes the first word in sentences and most common proper names. However, his or her use of more complex capitalization is spotty within dialogue, abbreviations, and proper names ("Aunt Maria" versus "my aunt," for instance).

D. **Applying Grammar and Usage:** The writer has made grammar and usage mistakes throughout the piece, but they do not interfere with the reader's ability to understand the message. Issues related to agreement, tense, and word usage appear here and there, but can be easily corrected.

score 3

Developing

score 2

LOW

Emerging

A. **Checking Spelling:** The writer has misspelled many words, even simple ones, which causes the reader to focus on conventions rather than on the central theme or storyline.

B. **Punctuating Effectively:** The writer has neglected to use punctuation, used punctuation incorrectly, and/or forgotten to indent paragraphs, making it difficult for the reader to find meaning.

C. **Capitalizing Correctly:** The writer uses capitals inconsistently even in common places such as the first word in a sentence. He or she uses capitals correctly in some places, but has no consistent control over them.

D. **Applying Grammar and Usage:** The writer makes frequent mistakes in grammar and usage, making it difficult to read and understand the piece. Issues related to agreement, tense, and word usage abound.

score 1

Rudimentary

PAPER #1: GRADE 3

What we think of the piece, based on points in the scoring guides:

Without question, this writer is writing from experience. Her topic is focused, and her details are accurate and relevant. Her low opinion of bees comes through not only in her words, but also in her tone. To top things off, the piece is well edited. The writer's spelling and use of capital letters and punctuation are strong. Therefore, she deserves kudos for ideas, voice, and conventions. Her organization, however, could be better. She makes it clear from the start that she does not like bees because they sting—and she ends the piece with the same message, along with the all-too-common line, "And that is why . . ." There is no momentum—no real thrust to the idea. We also wish she had chosen her words more carefully and courageously. The piece is a bare-bones explanation.

> Bees
>
> I do not like bees because it hurts when they sting. I hate their buzzing sound If you accidently hit theire nest, they will chase you. And if you try to shoe them a way they sting you. The main part I don't like about bees is theire stingers. And that why I don't like bees.

How we score this piece:

* Ideas: 5	Word Choice: 2
* Organization: 2	Sentence Fluency: 3
Voice: 4	* Conventions: 5

* Traits we choose to focus on in a conference.

Comments to the writer:

"Your piece tells me that you know a lot about what angers bees. It also suggests you've had a bad run-in or two with bees. Am I right? [Let the student answer.] Your experience has provided you with a great idea. How about folding in some of that experience to illustrate *why* you don't like bees? Rather than starting and ending with pretty much the same statement, start with something that will grab the reader—and end with something that will make sure he or she never forgets your piece. Your organization will shine! Your use of conventions is excellent. Be sure to continue applying them so well."

PAPER #2: GRADE 3

Football is a very fun sport. I just love to hit the snot out of people when I am mad at them. But it is not fun geting cloked by somone else on the other team. When they make me mad. I get **steamy** mad!

What we think of the piece, based on points in the scoring guides:

Can you imagine this kid on the football field? Heaven help the other team! To us, his passion comes through mainly in his word choice. Though quite unappetizing, phrases like "hitting the snot out of people" and "getting clocked by someone" capture the rough-and-tumble nature of the game perfectly. The piece flows well, too, largely because the writer begins and structures each sentence in a different way. It's weak, however, in ideas, not because it isn't focused—it most definitely is—but because it lacks details. Why does the writer enjoy football? What, specifically, makes him angry? How does his anger impact his game? Answering questions like these would add dimension to the piece.

How we score this piece:

*	Ideas: 3	*	Word Choice: 5
	Organization: 3	*	Sentence Fluency: 4
	Voice: 4		Conventions: 3

* Traits we choose to focus on in a conference.

Comments to the writer:

"It's so important for writers to write about their passions—and that's just what you've done here. You're passionate about football. I can tell by your word choice. [Point to phrases like "hitting the snot out of people" and "getting clocked by someone."] Your words are so colorful and natural. They put me in the game. Your sentence fluency is strong, too. I admire the way you start and structure each sentence differently. The piece flows. That said, I have questions about your idea: Why do you enjoy football? What makes you mad? How does your anger make you a better player? [Let the student answer.] Great! Why don't you weave in some of those details? As a reader, I'd really like to know them."

Chapter 2: Assessing Student Work

Scoring Guides

Sample Papers

Lessons

Activities

FAQs

PAPER #3: GRADE 3

What we think of the piece, based on points in the scoring guides:

This piece has "prompt" written all over it: "If you were planning Thanksgiving dinner, what would you serve?" And the writer completed the assignment. But that's all she did. She shows no connection whatsoever to the topic—and gives no indication that she cares about it. As a result, the piece lacks voice. The repetitive sentences (for the most part, all beginning with "I would cook . . .") provides further evidence of the writer's indifference to the topic. Her word choice is good, though. "Venison," "carrots," "oranges," and "pecan pie" give the reader a clear picture of the menu because those words are precise.

Comments to the writer:

"This piece is making me so hungry! Do you know why? Because your words are so precise. Instead of just saying "meat," you say "venison." Instead of just saying "dessert," you say "pecan pie." By choosing your words so carefully, you enable me, the reader, to see clearly each delicious menu item. It's not clear to me, though, why you picked these items. I suspect it's because they are your favorites, but that's not coming through in the writing. Is there a way to add your personal stamp? In other words, add more voice? You may want to try writing like you speak. Imagine telling your best friend what you're serving for Thanksgiving. What would that sound like? Write it down. By doing this, you'll not only add voice, but you'll bring more flow, or sentence fluency, to the piece. I can't wait to see your next draft."

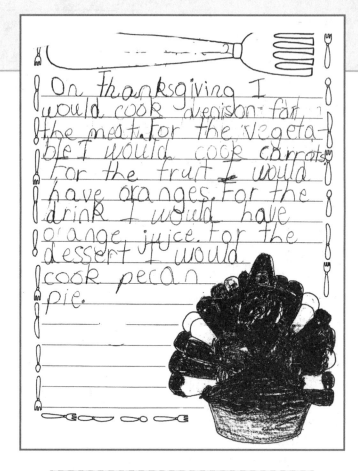

How we score this piece:

Ideas: 3

Organization: 2

* Voice: 1

* Word Choice: 5

* Sentence Fluency: 2

Conventions: 4

* Traits we choose to focus on in a conference.

PAPER #4: GRADE 4

What we think of the piece, based on points in the scoring guides:

This writer has certainly done his homework about the similarities and differences between penguins and pelicans. His idea is strong—and he includes so many rich, relevant details, which he organizes in a straightforward, sensible way. The reader walks away with a lot of good information about these birds. However, the piece lacks voice and sentence fluency. Like the writer of paper #3, this writer was most likely given a standard assignment—to write a comparison/contrast paper (for English class, as the title suggests), based on facts he collected in a Venn diagram. And he rose to the challenge.

Comments to the writer:

"You have done your research on penguins and pelicans, that's for sure. I'm so impressed by all the facts you give and the way you've organized them by discussing the birds' similarities in the first paragraph and their differences in the second. The piece is very easy to read because of your organization and excellent use of conventions. Now let's work on bringing your idea to life. You can do that in a couple of ways: In addition to facts about penguins and pelicans, include your thoughts and feelings about them. That will bring out your voice. And try to construct a few of your sentences in different ways so that they all don't feel so similar. [Show examples of similar sentences.] That will enhance your piece's fluency."

English

Penguins and Pelicans are alike in some way. One way they are alike is, they both are bird. Another way the birds are similar is they llive near the water. Also they both have feathers. Some more way they are alike are they both eut fish, lay eggs, and they both live in colonies (not like the 13 colonies).

Penguins and Pelicans also differ in ways also. A way that they are different is Pelicans can fly, but Penguins can not; they can only walk and swim. Also Pelicans have a huge pouch on their bills, and Penguins have small beaks. Another way the birds differ is Penguins are black and white, but Pelicans are white with brown, gray, or black. Some other ways they are different is Penguins swim veary fast under water, but Pelicans

swim on top of water, and Penguins live in cold climates, wh Pelicans live in warmer areas. Tha is how Penguins and Pelicans ar alike and different in many wa

---

How we score this piece:

* Ideas: 5	Word Choice: 4
Organization: 3	* Sentence Fluency: 2
* Voice: 2	Conventions: 4

* Traits we choose to focus on in a conference.

PAPER #5: GRADE 4

What we think of the piece, based on points in the scoring guides:

We respect what this student is trying to do: Persuade her classmates to read by writing about the value of reading in everyday life. The fact that she touches on the full range of texts available to us, from road signs to research materials, suggests that she truly understands the important role reading plays in school and beyond. So we give her high marks for ideas. However, the writing lacks a logical sense of direction. The details are strung together loosely at best. Further, the writer's mediocre use of conventions interferes with our ability to follow her argument and, in the end, buy it.

Comments to the writer:

"Something tells me you love to read. That's terrific! As you point out so clearly in your piece, reading serves many purposes—from preventing us from getting lost to helping us learn about things in our world (like animals). So your idea works. Do you feel it's also important to read for pleasure? [Let the student answer.] You may want to weave in that detail. From there, think about putting *all* your details in an order that makes sense to the reader. For example, combine your point about animals in the first paragraph with your point about knowing a lot about things in the third paragraph. Improving your organization that way will make the piece easier to read and even more persuasive. And, you clearly know how to use most conventions, so when you spot words that don't look right as you're revising, try to correct them. If you think your piece needs some heavy editing, save that for later. I'll help you."

> **Reading is Power**
>
> Reading is fun and gives you power if you read you can learn about stuff like animals. Today we went to a play this boy could not read his homwork but he trid and trid but at the end he could read. If you could read you could not read rode sings are you would get lost you have to read to get throw school if you didn't you would fell.
>
> reading is power becous if you read a lot about something you will no a lot about it. If you cant read you beeter learn to.

How we score this piece:

* Ideas: 4   Word Choice: 3

* Organization: 2   Sentence Fluency: 3

Voice: 3   * Conventions: 2

* Traits we choose to focus on in a conference.

PAPER #6: GRADE 4

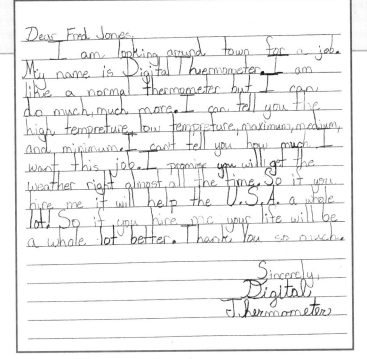

Dear Fred Jones,
I am looking around town for a job.
My name is Digital Thermometer. I am
like a normal thermometer but I can
do much, much more. I can tell you the
high tempreture, low temperature, maximum, medium,
and minimum. I can't tell you how much I
want this job. I promise you will get the
weather right almost all the time. So if you
hire me it will help the U.S.A. a whole
lot. So if you hire me your life will be
a whole lot better. Thank You so much.

Sincerely,
Digital
Thermometer

What we think of the piece, based on points in the scoring guides:

This student chose to become a digital thermometer (from a list of weather-forecasting tools) and write a letter of application to a meteorologist, explaining why he'd be the perfect hire. Although the assignment is a bit farfetched, we sense the student enjoyed carrying it out because his voice is strong. (Voice is usually a reliable indicator of the student's interest in an assignment.) Pride in his unique skills and qualities as a thermometer rings out. He makes a compelling argument, which is easy to follow because of his excellent use of conventions. Although the sentences are mechanically correct, though, they lack variety. Notice that all but the last two are nearly identical in length and begin with the word *I*. Therefore, we'd encourage work on sentence fluency.

How we score this piece:

Ideas: 3	Word Choice: 3
Organization: 4	* Sentence Fluency: 2
* Voice: 6	* Conventions: 5

* Traits we choose to focus on in a conference.

Comments to the writer:

"Your piece has all the elements of a strong letter of application: you explain why you are writing, why you would be perfect for the job, and how you would improve the quality of life for your employer. Your message is persuasive, in other words—and that comes through in your voice. I sense you really want the job *because* of your voice. You deserve high marks for conventions, too. Your grammar and mechanics are, for the most part, perfect, which makes reading your writing a pleasure. One way you could improve your piece is to bring more sentence variety to it. Notice how almost every one of your sentences is about the same length and begins with the word *I*. How about changing a couple to add interest and create rhythm?"

PAPER #7: GRADE 5

What we think of the piece, based on points in the scoring guides:

Although the beginning of this piece is far from bold and its ending far from excellent, its middle provides good, reliable, well-organized information about Eli Whitney. In fact, organizing biographies chronologically is a tried-and-true technique. Professional writers have been doing it for generations. So the main idea and organization are working—but the piece severely lacks details. The writer provides only bare-bones information about Eli Whitney. We want more. Although the writer begins and ends sentences clearly and uses some nice prepositional and transitional phrases, he doesn't vary them at all, making the piece easy to read, but lifeless.

How we score this piece:

* Ideas: 2	Word Choice: 3
* Organization: 4	Sentence Fluency: 2
* Voice: 2	Conventions: 4

* Traits we choose to focus on in a conference.

Comments to the writer:

"Eli Whitney is an important figure in history. Without a doubt, you got all your facts straight—and have organized them in a way that makes sense: chronologically. Good for you! At the same time, the piece leaves me with more questions than answers. Where was Eli born? In what year did he die? What is a cotton gin, and *why* did he invent it? Did it solve a problem for him and his community? If so, what was the problem? You say he became famous in his lifetime. Was he happy about that? Or was fame a burden? I'm asking a lot of questions, I know. But that's because you, as a writer, have piqued my curiosity. Answering questions like these will help you add details. It also might help you add variety to your sentences so that the subject of each one isn't *he* or *Eli Whitney.*"

PAPER #8: GRADE 5

What we think of the piece, based on points in the scoring guides:

It's interesting to compare this paper to the last one. Both were written by fifth graders. Both are about people in history. Both focus on significant events in the lives of those people. But the similarities end there. Unlike the last piece, this one contains some nice details such as "When I came through Ellis Island, my name was changed . . ." "I caught a glimpse of her and waved . . ." "I had to live in a boarding house . . ." There are also some nice moments of sentence fluency: "I remember when I first came to America. The year was 1890." Finally, the writer's superb use of conventions makes reading a pleasure. However, the organization needs work. The piece lacks a clear sense of direction. The details, as good as they may be, are strung together randomly. There is only a hint of internal structure.

> Hi my name is Meyer Yezierska. When I came through Ellis Island my name was changed to Max Mayer. I am Hattie's older brother. I have five family members that also came to America.
>
> I remember when I first came to America. The year was 1890. I had to meet my family at Ellis Island. I was trying to see my sister Anzia. I caught a glimpse of her and waved. She didn't know that my name had been changed because they couldn't pronounce it. I led my family across the streets of New York City. I had to live in a boarding house and sweatshops just like Anzia. My mother died and my father gave lessons to boys in Plotsk.
>
> I turned out to be very rich because of my job. I had traveled back to Plotsk with Anzia. Finally, I got married and had three children.

How we score this piece:

* Ideas: 4	Word Choice: 3
* Organization: 1	Sentence Fluency: 3
Voice: 4	* Conventions: 6

* Traits we choose to focus on in a conference.

Comments to the writer:

"Through your writing, you have become Max Mayer. Your ideas and voice particularly make me a believer. And your excellent use of conventions allowed me to read the piece with ease. Thank you. That said, I feel you've given snapshots of Max's life, rather than a full-blown movie. Think about organizing your fine details in a way that makes more sense. Maybe begin with why you came to America in the first place and from where, how you got here, how you felt when you arrived, and so forth. From there, explain what it was like meeting your family on Ellis Island, where you lived, where you worked, and your general impressions of America. You've already given the reader many of these details; now it's just a matter of structuring them more logically and adding more details as necessary to fill in any missing information in Max's amazing story."

PAPER #9: GRADE 5

What we think of the piece, based on points in the scoring guides:

Could this paper be any clearer or more focused? The writer knows what she wants to say—and says it, without wasting a word. She doesn't just state that she aspires to be an astronaut over an oceanographer, she explains why by providing compelling, convincing details. The words she has chosen, such as *gravity, explore, pollution, aliens,* and *planet,* bring details to life and are appropriate for the topic and audience. The piece stumbles a bit, though, when it comes to sentence fluency. It hums along steadily, but in a predictable, almost businesslike fashion. The writer could do more to make it sound more fluid and natural.

Comments to the writer:

"You are an excellent writer, and this piece proves it. After reading it, I had a clear sense of *why* you want to be an astronaut—to have fun, to apply all you've learned about outer space, to explore the effects of pollution, to look for other life forms and planets. Wow! There is real power in those details. There is also power in the words you chose because they tell me, the reader, that you know what you're talking about—words such as *gravity, explore, pollution, aliens,* and *planet.* Your sentences are composed correctly and support your details and words well. If you used more variety in your sentences, your work would be even stronger and more interesting to the reader. Try making some longer or shorter. Check to make sure they don't all start the same way. Then read your revision aloud to make sure it sounds more fluent."

"If I Could Choose"

If I could choose to be an astronaut or and oceangrapher, I would be an astronaut. Being an astronaut would be so much fun. And since I am only eleven years old, I would gather information about the benifits from space I have learned, that I can apply on Earth.

Just seeing Earth from space would make me want to float around for hours because there is no gravity. I would even explore the affects of pollution outside Earth. I would also try to look for other life, maybe aliens. I would try to find and explore a new planet that has never been seen before.

Being an astronaut would be cool. Except for having to be in collage from 4-8 years. I would deffinatly be too tired of school then.

How we score this piece:

* Ideas: 6	* Word Choice: 5
Organization: 4	* Sentence Fluency: 3
Voice: 4	Conventions: 4

* Traits we choose to focus on in a conference.

Concluding Thought

We can't stress this point enough: We must explain to writers, or help them to discover for themselves, the reasons a piece is or isn't working and what to do about it, regardless of where they fall on the developmental continuum. The traits enable us to do that. When we use the scoring guides to communicate clearly with students, they learn, right along with us, how writing works. We also come to know, specifically, what we need to teach. The next two chapters contain lessons and activities for you to use once you've taken that step—once you've assessed your students' work using the scoring guides and have determined where they need help the most.

Trait-Based Lessons for the Whole Class

There is no better way to introduce the traits than by gathering students together and exploring them as a group. This chapter contains whole-class lessons for each trait, organized by key quality, with clear directions for carrying them out. The lessons on ideas, organization, voice, word choice, and sentence fluency center on developing critical revision skills, while the lessons on conventions center on developing critical editing skills—spelling, punctuation, capitalization, and grammar and usage. We round out the chapter with tips for publishing to ensure that students' work looks as good as it reads.

We've provided enough lessons to use on a regular basis—24 total. But that doesn't mean you need to follow them sequentially. You should use them in whatever order you wish, in a way that makes sense for you and your students. The important thing is to carry all of them out by the year's end. You may first want to assess your students' writing using the trait scoring guides on pages 24–29. Doing so will reveal traits that your students struggle with most and help you choose appropriate lessons.

Guidelines for Conducting Lessons

Every teacher has his or her own way of planning and giving lessons, but here are some tips that have proven effective in our work:

1. Read the lesson beforehand to familiarize yourself with it, anticipate children's questions, and collect the necessary materials.

2. Gather the children around you, making sure that each one can see you and any materials you will be using.

3. Introduce the lesson by telling children the trait and key quality you're exploring and why they're essential to becoming a good writer. Use the high points on the scoring guides on pages 24–29 if you need ideas for what to say.

4. Work through each step of the lesson, taking your cue from the students to determine how much time to spend on it. If they "get it," move on. If they don't, stick with it, repeating procedures, asking questions, encouraging answers, and so forth.

5. Allow students to share their responses and discuss issues raised in the lesson. Don't be afraid to diverge a bit.

6. If time allows, encourage students to practice by giving them one of the activities on pages 86–103 or by choosing pieces from their writing folders to revise or edit.

Regardless of how you conduct the lessons, students should take what they learn and apply it to the extended pieces that they're working on during independent writing. Since students are revising and editing these pieces over time, they can apply what they learn as they learn it, which leads to thoughtful, polished final pieces. When students revise and edit their own work using the language of the traits, they come to understand how and when to revise and edit, regardless of the purpose for their writing. The sooner they begin using the tools that successful, independent writers use to improve their work, the sooner they'll become successful, independent writers themselves.

Ideas Lessons

The goal of assessment is to improve instruction so that students perform better each time they attempt a task. So let's build a bridge from assessment to instruction for the trait of ideas. There are four key qualities of the ideas trait that every student can learn:

❖ Finding a Topic

❖ Focusing the Topic

❖ Developing the Topic

❖ Using Details

In the pages that follow, we offer lessons for teaching these qualities. As you carry out the lessons, keep your focus on the trait, while linking lesson goals to your school and district's curriculum. And, of course, feel free to adapt the lessons by weaving in your own good thinking.

Scoring Guides

Sample Papers

Lessons

Activities

FAQs

| Lesson #1 | **FINDING A TOPIC** |

Ideas for writing pop up when we least expect them and, therefore, can be lost all too easily unless we have a place to capture them. In this lesson, students learn to use a writer's notebook, or "seed idea notebook," to think about and jot down possible topics for writing.

WHAT TO DO:

1. Show students a filled-in sample page of a writer's notebook. If you wish, you can use an overhead of the reproducible on page 44, filling in the four sections using words, phrases, questions, pictures, and lists to capture ideas for writing. Emphasize that taking the time to enter even the quickest notation can help us remember a good idea.

2. Hand out a copy of the Seed Idea Notebook to each student. Tell students that this is what they will use as their own writer's notebook. Discuss why it is called Seed Idea Notebook and that you hope they will use it to let writing ideas grow. Students can personalize the cover by coloring in the picture and adding their own words and art.

3. Tell students to capture three ideas in their notebooks, reminding them that they can use words, phrases, questions, pictures, and/or lists. They need to write down only enough to retain the idea for consideration later.

4. Ask students to choose one of the three ideas as the topic for a piece of writing. They may wish to discuss their choice with a neighbor. Give them paper and pencils, and let them start to work.

MATERIALS:

* an overhead transparency of the Seed Idea Notebook Pages reproducible (page 44)

* photocopies of the Seed Idea Notebook Cover reproducible (page 43) and the Seed Idea Notebook Pages reproducible (page 44): To create a notebook, cut apart covers and pages and staple together a cover, the 4 labeled notebook pages, and 2 blank pages behind each labeled page.

* writing paper

* pens or pencils

FOLLOW-UP ACTIVITIES:

* After students have used their notebooks over a period of time, have them review the contents and talk with a partner about possible writing topics. Ask members of the class to share their notebook entries and resulting pieces of writing. Emphasize how the seed idea in the notebook leads to a longer piece of writing. Every two weeks, or as time allows, ask students to share why ideas in their notebooks are special. As one student shares, another may get a new idea to include in his or her notebook.

* Read *Amelia's Notebook* (2006) by Marissa Moss, a clever picture book that shows students the range of items and entries that might find its way into a writer's notebook. It provides a concrete example of how a notebook helps a writer find good ideas.

Seed Idea Notebook Cover

Seed Idea Notebook

_____
writer's name

Seed Idea Notebook

_____
writer's name

Seed Idea Notebook

_____
writer's name

Seed Idea Notebook

_____
writer's name

Seed Idea Notebook Pages

Things I notice:

Things I wonder about:

Things that make me laugh:

Things that worry me:

Getting Started With the Traits: Grades 3–5 © 2009 Ruth Culham and Raymond Coutu, Scholastic.

Lesson #2 | FOCUSING THE TOPIC

This lesson gives students the opportunity to practice taking a big topic and focusing it to create a narrower, more manageable one. Specifically, students listen to Jon J. Muth's extraordinary book, *The Three Questions* (2002), use writing to find answers to the following questions, and, in the process, arrive at a "big idea" behind each one:

❊ When is the best time to do things?

❊ Who is the most important one?

❊ What is the right thing to do?

> **MATERIALS:**
>
> ❊ a copy of *The Three Questions* by Jon J. Muth
>
> ❊ small index cards, three per student
>
> ❊ writing paper
>
> ❊ pens or pencils

WHAT TO DO:

1. Give each student three index cards and ask them to label each at the top with one of these three questions: *When is the best time to do things? Who is the most important one? What is the right thing to do?*

2. Allow time for students to write a one- or two-sentence answer to each question on the cards. Have them draw a line under their answer. For example, for "When is the best time to do things?" a student might write, "In the morning when you are fresh." Or, "Right away when you are thinking about it so you don't forget." Have the class share responses and discuss.

3. Read *The Three Questions* and stop after page 6, which reads, "'Fighting,' barked Pushkin right away."

4. Ask students to write more about each question underneath the line on the front of their index card. This time when they write, expect to see more thoughtful answers focused on a big idea. As they think about the ideas in the story, students get a chance to write at a deeper level, getting right to the heart of the main idea.

5. Finish reading *The Three Questions*. Direct students to use the back of their index cards to write reactions to Muth's answer for each question. Ask students to write about any surprises they experienced in Muth's answers—and/or have them compare Muth's answers to each of their own answers and discuss their pieces as a class.

FOLLOW-UP ACTIVITIES:

❊ Have students create skits based on the pieces they write, demonstrating the importance of the three questions in everyday life at school.

❊ Read Tolstoy's original short story "The Three Questions" and explore the way Muth changed the characters and details, yet maintained the original theme.

| Lesson #3 | **DEVELOPING THE TOPIC** |

In *The Secret Knowledge of Grown-Ups* (1998), David Wisniewski explains all the "secret" rules that grown-ups follow but conceal from children. The result is a book that overflows with humor, energy, and imagination. In this lesson, students write their own secret rules—a wonderful way to learn how to develop a topic.

WHAT TO DO:

1. Read *The Secret Knowledge of Grown-Ups* to the class and discuss the key ideas that the author uses to intrigue the reader.

2. Review the trait of ideas with students, showing why the author would score high in developing his topic.

3. Lead the class in a discussion about "secret rules" that most kids have to follow, such as eating their vegetables and combing their hair. Write students' ideas on a transparency. Then choose one or two ideas that small groups or pairs can write about on their own.

4. Discuss the voice that they think will work the best. Explore the differences between a kid's voice in writing and an adult's voice.

5. Look at the patterns of organization in *The Secret Knowledge of Grown-Ups* to help students decide on an organization to fit their "secret rule" idea.

6. Allow plenty of time for students to write their piece and illustrate it with markers, paints, magazine cut-outs, and so on. Be sure to plan time to share their final work.

FOLLOW-UP ACTIVITIES:

*   Create collections of "secret rules" books and share them with other classes.

*   Have students use their writer's notebooks to keep a running list of possible new rules for future writing topics.

MATERIALS:

*   a copy of *The Secret Knowledge of Grown-Ups* by David Wisniewski
*   overhead transparencies and markers
*   writing paper
*   pens or pencils
*   markers, paints
*   magazines to cut up

Lesson #4   USING DETAILS

I n *Nothing Ever Happens on 90th Street* (1997), Roni Schotter addresses the age-old complaint: "I have nothing to write about." Young Eva wanders through her neighborhood, soliciting advice on topics for a class assignment. Everyone from the fish salesman to the limousine driver offers delightful words of wisdom:

MATERIALS:

❖ a copy of *Nothing Ever Happens on 90th Street* by Roni Schotter

❖ a checklist of tasks (below)

❖ book-making supplies: large sheets of white paper, magazines to cut up, markers, pens, pencils, glue, tape, scissors

❖ Write about what you know.

❖ Find the poetry: a new way with old words.

❖ Use your imagination.

❖ Ask, "What if?"

❖ Add a little action.

❖ And, yes, observe carefully and don't forget the details.

The result is a picture book that could be the focus of an entire course on writing.

WHAT TO DO:

1. Read aloud and discuss *Nothing Ever Happens on 90th Street*.

2. Give students a checklist of at least ten tasks to do around the school and tell them to check off each one as they accomplish it. They should spend no more than two minutes on each activity. Here is what your checklist might look like:

❖ Take a seat inside the media center.

❖ Hang out in the music room.

❖ Sit at a table in the cafeteria.

❖ Check out the action in the back foyer.

❖ Watch a gym class.

❖ See what is happening in the art room.

❖ Visit a classroom you've never seen before.

❖ Follow the secretary or the custodian for two minutes.

❖ Observe a class at recess.

❖ Count the number of cars that pull in and out of the parking lot.

Scoring Guides
Sample Papers
Lessons
Activities
FAQs

3. Stagger where students start and request that they follow the sequence of tasks on the checklist to avoid overcrowding at individual locations. Ask them to record information about each place—the sights, the sounds, the feel, the people—on their own.

4. Encourage students to gather two or three interesting details about their observations at each station and record them on their checklist. Invite them to illustrate their details, just like Eva does in the story. Remind them to be "invisible" and courteous during their visits and to follow the advice of Eva's 90th Street neighbors.

5. Have students share their details when they return to the classroom. From there, ask them to write, illustrate, and bind "Nothing Ever Happens at [the name of your school]" stories of their own to display in the library or media center for schoolmates to enjoy. Be sure to put a copy of Schotter's book next to the student-written books so readers see how picture books inspire good writing.

FOLLOW-UP ACTIVITY:

- Ask students to repeat this exercise at home, noting all the little things about everyday life on their street.

Organization Lessons

Now let's explore strategies for building skills in organization—or the internal structure of the piece. We're specifically concerned with these key qualities:

- Creating the Lead
- Using Sequence Words
- Structuring the Body
- Ending With a Sense of Resolution

Part of being able to organize well is knowing how to lay out the details that guide the reader through the text. If the writer doesn't do that, it is enormously frustrating to the reader. The writer can't just let the details loose to head down an unpredictable trail. Who knows where the reader will end up?! Writing needs to be more of a highway that gets the readers to where they want to go, as they take in some interesting scenery, explore new terrain, and discover new things along the way.

Lesson #1 · CREATING THE LEAD

When a paper begins, "I'm going to tell you about . . ." readers hit the snooze button. But when it begins, "Bang! I woke up and wondered what on earth was going on," readers pay attention. They want to know where the writer is going. What follows is a lesson for helping students kick off their writing with a bang.

MATERIALS:

✲ 30 to 40 large index cards and pens or pencils

✲ a 2-inch loose-leaf ring

✲ an overhead transparency of the techniques and examples below

WHAT TO DO:

1. Write the following techniques for creating bold beginnings on the front of individual index cards, then write or draw the examples on the back.

Lights, Camera, Action—The writer makes something happen.
Example: "For the last time," my dad said. "Put your gum here."

Single Word—The writer sets off an important word by itself and follows it up with more information.
Example: Gum. Gum was everywhere. It was in my hair. It was in the carpet. It was on my pillow.

Fascinating Fact—The writer presents an intriguing piece of information.
Example: I blew a bubble bigger than my brother's head.

Imagine This—The writer captures a moment in words or pictures.
Example: The gum made my bangs stick straight out from my head.

It's Just My Opinion—The writer states a belief.
Example: Kids should be able to chew gum any time they want.

Listen Up—The writer describes a sound.
Example: Smack, snap, slurp.

I Wonder—The writer asks a question or a series of questions.
Example: Have you ever wondered how many pieces of gum will fit into the human mouth? Five? Ten? More?

2. Arrange students in groups of three or four. Give each group a card.

3. Have a member of each group read the techniques and the examples. Then tell groups to come up with another example.

4. Ask groups to write the new examples on the cards. Encourage students to add pictures if they think it will clarify the message.

5. Prepare an overhead transparency of the original list of techniques and examples. Read them one at a time and ask each group to share its new lead and the technique on which it's based. Be sure all groups have a chance to share.

6. Collect the cards and punch a hole in the top left corner of each for binding with the loose-leaf ring. Put this ring of leads in the writing center as a resource for students when they can't think of a way to begin future work.

7. Encourage students to add techniques and examples to the ring as they think of them.

| Lesson #2 | **USING SEQUENCE WORDS** |

In *The Secret Shortcut* (1996), Wendell and Floyd are prone to telling some pretty tall tales about why they are late to school. Aliens, pirates, and a plague of frogs are excuses tried but discarded because their teacher doesn't believe them. So the boys commit to getting to school on time by taking a shortcut, which turns out to be more of a problem than a solution. In this two-session lesson, students create their own "shortcut stories," using sequence words and phrases to guide the reader.

MATERIALS:

❊ a copy of *The Secret Shortcut* by Mark Teague

❊ chart paper

❊ writing paper

❊ pens or pencils

❊ markers and drawing/ construction paper

WHAT TO DO ON DAY 1:

1. Read *The Secret Shortcut* aloud.

2. Discuss and list on chart paper all the things that happen to Wendell and Floyd on the way to school. Hang the list in a prominent place so all students can see and refer to it.

3. Give groups of two or three students a large piece of drawing/construction paper and have them draw a map containing a brand-new shortcut to school for Wendell and Floyd. Encourage students to expand on the text by including things the characters might encounter along the way, such as volcanoes, quicksand, and bottomless pits.

WHAT TO DO ON DAY 2:

1. Discuss the student-created maps as a prewriting activity.

2. Ask the small groups to create new "Secret Shortcut" stories based on their maps, using a sentence starter such as, "Wendell and Floyd took a new shortcut to school," if you wish.

3. Discuss sequence words and phrases that can help organize the events in the story, such as:

before	*first*	*first of all*	*in turn*
after	*second*	*to begin with*	*later on*
then	*third*	*in the first place*	*meanwhile*
next	*earlier*	*at the same time*	*soon*
during	*later*	*for now*	*in the meantime*
finally	*now*	*for the time being*	*while*
sometimes	*last*	*the next step*	*simultaneously*
often	*at first*	*in time*	*afterward*

4. Have groups write at least three detailed sentences to describe each event on the map.

5. Tell students to describe each event in a paragraph that begins with a sequence word or phrase. For example, if the map shows a bottomless pit, they might begin the paragraph this way: "After reaching the bottomless pit, Wendell and Floyd tiptoed around the edges, trying frantically not to fall in. The pit was dark, shadowy, and seemed as though it was reaching out to grab them as they tried to sneak by."

FOLLOW-UP ACTIVITY:

❖ Have groups find examples of sequence words and phrases in other texts and talk about how they help link details and events. Ask students to make a chart with the words and phrases, with examples of how to use them. Hang the chart in the classroom. Then have students look through other picture books to find strong and obvious organizational patterns that really work.

| Lesson #3 | **STRUCTURING THE BODY** |

Franklin D. Roosevelt's statement "The only thing we have to fear is fear itself" may have soothed a nation, but it didn't do a thing for the title character in *Scaredy Squirrel* (2006), because he is afraid of everything—particularly germs, sharks, tarantulas, poison ivy, killer bees, and green Martians. So he never strays from his nut tree. That is, until the day he is visited by an unwelcome guest and, while diving for his emergency kit, makes a surprising discovery about himself. Mélanie Watt's interplay of text and visuals is fascinating. She combines elements of fiction (plot, characters, and so on) with elements of nonfiction (lists, charts, schedules, plans, and so on), proving that good organization is not only achieved through words, sentences, and paragraphs. In this lesson, students create their own lists, schedules, plans, and charts, using Watts's sweet, lively book as a model.

> **MATERIALS:**
>
> ❊ a copy of *Scaredy Squirrel* (2006) by Mélanie Watt
> ❊ slips of paper
> ❊ a box or hat
> ❊ chart paper and markers

WHAT TO DO:

1. Read *Scaredy Squirrel* to the class.

2. Brainstorm with the class a list of things Scaredy Squirrel writes about that shows his personality: (a) greatest fears, (b) benefits and drawbacks of change (leaving nut tree), (c) daily routine, (d) emergency kit contents, and (e) emergency exit plan.

3. Discuss the ways each type of writing in the book is organized:

    ❊ a list of items on a common topic

    ❊ a chart comparing two items to show differences or similarities

    ❊ a schedule or timeline

    ❊ a step-by-step plan to solve a problem

4. Write each type of organization on a slip of paper and place it into a box or hat.

5. Arrange the students into small groups and have one person from each group draw a slip and read it to the group. This will be the organization for the upcoming group writing. Replace the slips of paper in the box before the next group draws so all groups have the same options.

6. Ask each group to come up with a new list, chart, schedule, or plan, depending on what its slip says: (a) things they do well in school, or (b) things they like and don't like about going to school, or (c) a schedule of their school day, or (d) a step-by-step plan to get out of the classroom in case of an emergency. Give students time to record their writing on a large sheet of chart paper and ask them to draw pictures to illustrate their ideas.

7. Share what each group wrote and how members organized their ideas. Compare the differences and similarities of how each piece is organized.

Follow-Up Activities:

- Discuss with students what makes the organization of writing such as that found in *Scaredy Squirrel* different from a story or good information book. Emphasize the different ways of organizing for different purposes to make the ideas stand out.
- Share Mélanie Watt's sequel to *Scaredy Squirrel*, *Scaredy Squirrel Makes a Friend* (2006), and discuss how it is organized.

Lesson #4 Ending With a Sense of Resolution

Wrapping up a piece of writing is a challenge. Ask any writer. That's probably why a lot of young students cap theirs off with something like, "Now you know three reasons why hippopotamuses are ferocious," "I hope you liked my story," or the perennial favorite, "The end." What's reassuring, though, is that writers have choices.

In Barbara Abercrombie's *Charlie Anderson* (1995), the reader gets not one, not two, but three choices of ending. Charlie Anderson, a very fat, gray-striped cat, has it made. He gets to live in two houses with two families who love him. During the day, he eats and sleeps at one house. During the night, he does the same at the other house. But neither family knows it is sharing the cat. Both families think "their" cat is out hunting when he's not home, and it's only through a creative surprise ending, which works on several levels, that the truth is revealed.

Materials:

- a copy of *Charlie Anderson* by Barbara Abercrombie
- an overhead transparency and markers

What to Do:

1. Ask students, "What are some of the things authors do to signal to readers that they are wrapping things up?" Write students' ideas on the overhead. Their list may include "The End," "Thank you for reading my story," or "And then I woke up, and it was only a dream." They may also come up with more original ideas such as, "Since that day, I've never eaten green food." Discuss how effective each of these endings is and how important it is to conclude writing with a powerful thought, an image, or an idea that makes the reader think.

2. Show students *Charlie Anderson* and tell them it has three endings and one of them is a surprise.

3. Read the book aloud, pausing to show the pictures. When you come to the end, read the last three pages—the three endings—and let the last one sink in. Then ask, "Did this ending surprise anyone? Where in the story did the writer give us a little hint that set up this ending?"

4. Discuss how there's usually a clue to surprise endings earlier in the text so that the ending, while a surprise, makes sense. For example, early on, Abercrombie explains that Elizabeth and Sarah often visit their dad and stepmother in the city. So, when the story ends with the conclusion that the cat and the girls are lucky to have two families who love them, the reader thinks, "Oh, yeah!" This ending reveals the theme: There are other ways to love and be loved outside of a traditional family. Although intermediate writers most likely couldn't create endings as powerful as Abercrombie's, it's never too early to point them in the right direction.

5. Revisit the book's two other possible endings. In the first, the problem of who owns the cat is diplomatically resolved by renaming him Charlie Anderson, a combination of the names he was called by each family who thought he was exclusively theirs. The second ending deepens the reader's experience of the story. It becomes personal when one of the girls asks Charlie Anderson to declare which family he loves best.

6. Read the story again, focusing on the three endings. Pause after each, letting the artistry of the writer sink in.

7. Encourage students to look at the endings in other high-quality books. Do the authors wrap up the story convincingly, dig deep, or work with a big idea?

Voice Lessons

Can you teach voice? Our short answer: Yes! Although you can't focus on something as concrete as beginnings, middles, and endings as you can with organization, you can do many things to build awareness of the critical role voice plays in writing. You can engage students in activities that build skills in recognizing voice in the writing of others and in applying it to their own. Stories, essays, poems, lyrics, brochures, advertisements, posters, memos—all forms of writing contain voice and, therefore, are worth examining. And once students see the powerful influence voice has on those forms of writing, they'll be more inclined to use it in their own writing. This section shows you how to help them do just that by focusing on these key qualities:

❊ Establishing a Tone

❊ Conveying the Purpose

❊ Creating a Connection to the Audience

❊ Taking Risks to Create Voice

| Lesson #1 | **ESTABLISHING A TONE** |

MATERIALS:

❊ a copy of *Wolf!* by Becky Bloom

❊ a copy of "The Three Little Pigs" (any traditional version)

❊ overhead transparencies and markers

❊ writing paper

❊ pens or pencils

Voice jumps out when the point of view from which a story is being told changes. Famous fairy tales are excellent models for demonstrating this because they typically contain very familiar characters with very divergent personalities and perspectives. Becky Bloom's *Wolf!* (1999), a take-off on "The Three Little Pigs," is one example of many picture books in which the author creates a new story from an old one by shifting the point of view from the victims to the villain.

WHAT TO DO:

1. Discuss the genre of fairy tales with the class. Ask students to name their favorites and talk about the familiar characters in them, such as the mean wolf and the frightened little girl in "Little Red Riding Hood."

2. Read "The Three Little Pigs" aloud and then ask students to identify the voices they noticed. Are they warm and friendly? Distant and menacing? Somber? Humorous? See if students can pinpoint the most prominent voice.

3. Read *Wolf!* aloud and then discuss the similarities and differences between it and "The Three Little Pigs." Were the characters the same in both stories? Did both tales contain the same plotline, including the beginning and ending? What about the setting?

4. Ask students to identify the voice in *Wolf!* Is it the same as or different from the one used in "The Three Little Pigs"? If students feel it's different, ask them *how* it is different.

5. Create a chart on the overhead that compares the voices in the two books. Here's what it might look like:

Voices From *Wolf!*	Voices From "The Three Little Pigs"
patronizing	honest
aloof	scared
confident	nervous
positive	determined

6. Arrange students in small groups. Ask each group to select a traditional fairy tale and write a new version from the perspective of a different character, just as Bloom did. Remind students to pay close attention to the voice in which they write.

FOLLOW-UP ACTIVITIES:

❖ Encourage students to illustrate their stories and share them with younger students at school.

❖ Turn the stories into scripts and have students perform them. Be sure to allow plenty of time for rehearsal beforehand to build confidence and reading fluency.

Lesson #2 | **CONVEYING THE PURPOSE**

Students need to understand that knowing their purpose for writing is a key to choosing the right voice. For example, when a student writes a thank-you note to a grandparent, he or she typically uses a voice that expresses gratitude, appreciation, and love. However, if the same student writes to a toy company about a robot that broke the first time he or she played with it, that student would most likely use a voice that expresses frustration, disappointment, and even anger. In this lesson, students redesign a home's floor plan to get an important message about writing: choosing the right voice requires understanding one's purpose for writing.

MATERIALS:

❖ a simple floor plan of a house, apartment, or other residential building (Contact a local architectural firm or contractor to obtain copies at no cost.)

❖ paper, markers, pencils, crayons

WHAT TO DO:

1. Arrange students in groups of three or four. Give each group a copy of a floor plan. Ask each group to find the kitchen, bathroom, bedrooms, living room, laundry room, dining area, and family room.

2. Have each group select a room for an "extreme voice makeover." Tell them to radically change the room's size, shape, window locations, door locations, and so on, to make it more functional. In order to do this, it will be important for students to think about how the room was used—and could be used, given their changes. Have groups draw a picture of what the room looked like before the makeover and after it. Encourage students to emphasize how much the room has changed.

3. Attach their pictures to the floor plans.

4. Ask students to describe the room before and after the makeover. They may say, "The kitchen had no counter space, so we put an island in the middle of it . . . with a built-in cotton candy maker!"

5. Have students write a description of the person they think would use the new room, matching their design decisions to the person's personality.

6. Ask students how redesigning a room to meet a specific purpose is like writing to meet a specific purpose. And how does writing to meet a specific purpose relate to the trait of voice? Record their ideas on a chart and discuss them.

Lesson #3   CREATING A CONNECTION TO THE AUDIENCE

To a large extent, writing with voice means writing with emotion. A young mother's memoir about having a baby may be joyful. A commuter's editorial about rising gas prices may be angry. A soldier's letter from the front lines may be cheerful, but tinged with sadness and even fear. *Yesterday I Had the Blues* (2003) is full of emotion, as described by a young boy who starts out with the blues, but winds up with the "greens" (hopeful). His daddy has the "grays" (tense), his mama has the "reds" (annoyed), his sister has the "pinks" (cheerful), and so forth. By the end, we realize what the boy truly has is a real family with real feelings. In this lesson, students talk about a time they had the blues, as well as the greens, grays, reds, pinks, and so forth. From there, they put their ideas on paper. You'll be amazed at how colorful their voices can be.

MATERIALS:

- a copy of *Yesterday I Had the Blues* by Jeron Ashford Frame
- writing paper
- pencils, crayons, markers
- magazines to cut up

WHAT TO DO:

1. Ask students to think about the mood they were in when they woke up. Were they in a good mood, looking forward to going to school? Or, were they in a bad mood, wishing they could roll over and go back to sleep? Perhaps they were feeling yet another way?

2. Have them talk to a partner about their mood and select a color that matches it. If they were happy, for instance, they might pick bright green or yellow. If they were sad, they might choose gray, brown, or black. Encourage them to match their mood to a color as closely as they can.

3. Read *Yesterday I Had the Blues* to the class, showing the pictures as you go.

4. Ask students to name the mood of each character and how they identified it. Their answers should include the color that the author used as well as his description of the character.

5. Instruct students to talk to their partner again about the mood they were in when they got ready for school and refine their thoughts, based on *Yesterday I Had the Blues*.

6. Ask students to write about and illustrate on paper their mood, explaining the color they think best reflects that mood and why they chose it.

7. Share the mood pieces with the class and discuss them. Explain to students that writing should capture mood, or voice, to help the reader feel what the writer is feeling.

FOLLOW-UP ACTIVITIES:

❊ Help students create a book of colors and moods. Print lists of colors from the Internet and ask students to attach a mood to each one. Then bind the lists as a book for student to consult when they write.

❊ Share *The Sound of Colors: A Journey of the Imagination* (2006) by Jimmy Liao and discuss how the author describes colors. Ask students to discuss the book's voice and how color helped them to identify that voice.

Lesson #4 | TAKING RISKS TO CREATE VOICE

To create writing with voice—writing that speaks directly to the reader—students must take risks. In other words, they must express ideas in interesting, original ways. They must try things that few writers have tried before. They must experiment. By doing so, they arrive at a voice that is appropriate for their audience. In this lesson, students take risks by writing about one idea from various points of view.

> **MATERIALS:**
> * chart paper or overhead transparencies and markers
> * writing paper
> * pens or pencils

WHAT TO DO:

1. Write the following voiceless piece on chart paper or an overhead transparency and read it aloud to the class:

    "Rip in the Pants" by a fourth grader

    Just about a week ago my teacher had a rip in his pants. It was really funny. I didn't see it right away but someone told me then I saw it and wanted to laugh but I held it in. Then someone told him and everyone started to laugh. Then he went home to change.

    The End.

    Discuss students' reaction to the piece.

2. Divide the class into small groups and, on chart paper or a transparency, jot down possible points of view for the writing:

    * the student
    * the principal
    * the teacher
    * another teacher
    * a student who likes the teacher
    * a student who dislikes the teacher
    * the pants

3. Assign a point of view to each group of students and ask members to brainstorm ideas about how the voice would be different if the piece had been written from that point of view. For instance, what would the voice sound like if a student wrote about a teacher's pants ripping instead of the teacher himself writing about it?

4. Ask groups to rewrite the piece in the voice they feel is most appropriate. Three examples to share follow.

From the point of view of a student in the class:
Last week, my teacher Mr. Carroll had a colossal tear in the back of his pants. It happened when his pants got caught on the chalkboard edge. At first, I didn't notice it, but then my friend told me. We wanted to laugh at his bright pink boxers. We giggled, and he asked us what was so funny. We told him, and his face turned brighter than his boxers. He ran to the office to get Mrs. Holladay to sub for a while as he ran home to get changed. The whole class burst into laughter, and people had tears falling down their cheeks. We talked about it for the rest of the class. The next day, Mr. Carroll was very quiet and stayed as far away as possible from the chalkboard. He told us not to tell anyone. He would be the laughing stock of the school, the punch line in the teachers' lounge! Too late.

From the point of view of the teacher:
Rip! I didn't think much of it. Kids are always ripping something. I continued to teach. Giggle, snicker, snicker. I didn't think much of it. Students get off task. I addressed the giggling, and continued to teach. I felt a draft. I didn't think much of it, until I realized there shouldn't be a draft, especially there. I continued to teach. Then, a slow tingling, horrifying realization. The rip was from me and my pants—in a place it shouldn't be. The laughs were at me and my new drafty trousers. The red burned slowly from my neck to my forehead. My eyes met theirs. "Well," I said, "just get over it."

From the point of view of the pants:
This is not right. I wasn't made to be worn by a guy this big. Oww! Every time he does anything but stand still, I hurt. I'm packed, pulled, and stretched so tight I can hardly breathe. I need relief. What I really want is revenge. I know . . . I'll rip! Ha! That'll show him. But wait, what happens next? Maybe he'll just throw me out, and I'll never see the light of day again. Man, oh, man, why couldn't I be a tie? That way, I could choke him!

5. When students have finished, have a volunteer from each group read their piece aloud. Then ask the rest of the class to identify the voice and discuss whether it's appropriate for the person or thing speaking.

FOLLOW-UP ACTIVITIES:

❖ Read a picture book and have students think of how the voice might change if the story were told from various characters' points of view.

❖ Encourage students to explore all the possible voices for pieces they're working on. Once they've pinpointed an appropriate voice, have them add details that bring it out.

Word Choice Lessons

English is a complicated language, and it is easy for students to get lost in it. Intermediate students need help using familiar words in their writing and trying new ones. Reading to them, asking them questions about language, and piquing their curiosity about words will help students understand why it's important to find "just right" words as we write. The next section will help you do that. It contains lessons organized according to the following key qualities:

* Applying Strong Verbs

* Selecting Striking Words and Phrases

* Using Specific and Accurate Words

* Choosing Words That Deepen Meaning

Lesson #1	**APPLYING STRONG VERBS**

Word choice is about using rich, colorful, precise language that communicates not just in a functional way, but also in a moving and enlightening way. In this lesson, students explore the role of verbs in *Into the A, B, Sea* (2001), a delightful, rhyming book about sea animals, and then create their own books about land animals. In the process, they see just how powerful applying strong verbs can be.

MATERIALS:

* a copy of *Into the A, B, Sea* by Deborah Lee Rose

* drawing paper

* markers, crayons, paints

* animal pictures cut from magazines or printed out from Web sites

WHAT TO DO:

1. Read *Into the A, B, Sea* to students, showing the pictures as you go.

2. Ask students to tell you which animals' actions were the most interesting to them and explain why. Point out the verb Rose used for each of those animals. Remind students that choosing the right verbs—verbs that capture the action perfectly—can make a piece of writing enticing, interesting, and memorable.

3. Ask students to recall for you any of the animals whose actions surprised them or stuck in their minds. Point out the precision of the verb in each case and why such precision is characteristic of memorable writing.

4. Tell students you're going to reread the book, but this time you want them to write down six of their favorite animals and their actions—for example, *anemones sting, barnacles cling; octopuses hide, penguins glide; sea stars grab, tiger sharks nab.*

5. When you've finished reading, ask students to share their animals and verbs. Then tell them they are going to use powerful verbs to write about land animals, the way Rose does about sea animals in her book.

6. Assign students individual letters of the alphabet and ask them to use print and electronic resources to find an animal that begins with that letter—one that lives in the forest, in the jungle, or on the plains.

7. Pair up students and have them brainstorm verbs that describe their animals' actions. For example, "Aardvarks burrow, amble, forage, and lick." If a student isn't sure of typical actions for an animal, demonstrate how to find that information in books or on the Internet.

8. From their lists of possibilities, tell students to select their favorite verb—the one that sounds good and captures the animal's action precisely, such as "aardvarks amble," and consider synonyms for that verb, such as *shuffle, meander,* and *stroll.*

9. Ask students to write the name of their animal and its action on a sheet of drawing paper, along with a sentence that contains those two words—for example, "Aardvarks amble across the plains, looking for a tasty meal of grubs." Then, ask them to include a list of synonyms they considered: *shuffle, meander, stroll.* And, finally, have them illustrate their animal in action, using markers, crayons, paints, and pictures cut from magazines or printed out from Web sites.

10. Bind the pictures together to make a class book entitled *ABC Land Animals*—or hang the pictures alphabetically in a prominent place in the classroom or hallway.

11. Discuss with students what this lesson taught them about applying strong verbs. Give students time to talk to a partner and then ask for volunteers to share key qualities of the word choice trait. Record these qualities on the board or on a chart for students to consider when working on future writing projects.

Lesson #2 | SELECTING STRIKING WORDS AND PHRASES

The main character in *Fancy Nancy* (2006) is fancy. She likes to wear fancy clothes, eat fancy food, and, most of all, use fancy words like *chauffeur, plume,* and *merci.* However, her family is not fancy. Her mom, dad, and sister are perfectly content wearing T-shirts, eating ice-cream cones, and using ordinary words like *driver, feather,* and *thanks.* So Nancy takes it upon herself to educate them about the finer things in life by giving them a formal lesson, which ends in a wild game of dress-up. Then, to her delight, her dad suggests dinner out at the finest pizza joint in town. All heads turn when Nancy and her family enter the restaurant still wearing their flamboyant getups. "They probably think we're movie stars," Nancy muses. But then an embarrassing incident occurs, forcing her to rethink her priorities. In the lesson, students get a chance to look closely at Nancy's word choices and then try their hand at using fancy words of their own.

> **MATERIALS:**
>
> ❖ a copy of *Fancy Nancy* by Jane O'Connor
>
> ❖ chart paper and markers
>
> ❖ photocopies of the "Plain" Words List (page 64)
>
> ❖ photocopies of the "Fancy" Words List (page 64)

WHAT TO DO:

1. Read *Fancy Nancy* to students, pausing to point out some of the more interesting words as you read.

2. On the chart paper, make a list of the "fancy" words from the text: *fuchsia, plume, stupendous, accessories, posh, chauffeur, parfaits,* and *dressing gown.*

3. Ask students to tell you what the fancy words mean in plain English. Then write their responses next to each word. Encourage students to use the story context to guess the meaning of the fancy words if they are unfamiliar.

4. Discuss why authors are careful about choosing just-right words and how those words make the ideas more interesting.

5. Make photocopies of the "Fancy" Words List and "Plain" Words List. Cut them apart so that single words are on individual strips.

6. Divide the class in half. Give one "fancy" word to each student in one group. Give a "plain" word to each student in the other group.

7. Tell students that they have two minutes to find their word's partner. They should move around the room, calling out their word until they find a match. If students with "fancy" words ask for help, consult the master list at the top of the next page and give synonyms to help them figure out the meaning of their word.

Master List

bad: ghastly	big: enormous
good: delightful	cool: marvelous
happy: blissful	fast: swift
blue: turquoise	lazy: sluggish
sad: gloomy	hard: challenging
run: gallop	nice: pleasing
pretty: glamorous	walk: stroll

8.   When students have found their matching word, ask them to sit down so that they don't distract others who are continuing to look.

9.   Once all the students have found their matching word, ask them to come up in pairs to record their words on the chart paper under the headings "fancy" and "plain."

10.   Ask students if they have any favorite "fancy" words and, if so, encourage students to write them in their writer's notebooks to use in their own writing later.

"Plain" Words List

bad	happy
sad	blue
run	pretty
big	good
cool	fast
lazy	hard
nice	walk

"Fancy" Words List

ghastly	blissful
gloomy	turquoise
gallop	glamorous
enormous	delightful
marvelous	swift
sluggish	challenging
pleasing	stroll

| Lesson #3 | **USING SPECIFIC AND ACCURATE WORDS** |

Choosing the right words is essential to writing well, but learning how to do that takes time and practice. In this lesson, students examine a fascinating and fun nonfiction book, *Blood & Gore Like You've Never Seen!* (1997), for its specific and accurate use of scientific words. As you read the book aloud, students listen for unfamiliar words and use context clues to arrive at their meanings. From there, they create a poster using some of the specific and accurate words they learned from the book.

> **MATERIALS:**
>
> ❋ a copy of *Blood & Gore Like You've Never Seen!* by Vicki Cobb
>
> ❋ overhead transparencies and marker
>
> ❋ a photocopy of each of the following passages from the book: Blood, Skin, Bone , Muscle, Nerves, Digestion, Respiration
>
> ❋ poster board
>
> ❋ markers

WHAT TO DO:

1. Explain to students that you are going to read to them part of *Blood & Gore Like You've Never Seen!*, which contains lots of scientific facts about the human body— in particular about blood, skin, bone, muscle, nerves, and the digestive and respiratory systems. Read the table of contents aloud and ask students to vote on which section you will read.

2. Once a winner has been declared, ask students to call out any scientific words or phrases they anticipate will be included in the section. Record those words on a transparency entitled "Words and Phrases From *Blood & Gore.*"

3. Show students the pictures that go with the passage they selected. Explain that an electron microscope was used to capture these photographs, sometimes magnifying parts of the human body millions of times.

4. Read the section aloud. When you have finished, ask students to recall some of the words or phrases that stuck in their minds and record them on the transparency.

5. Ask students to go back to the list of words and phrases and identify any that are scientific. Put a star next to those words and phrases.

6. Tell students to look at the list again and identify words or phrases that are not scientific but are memorable or interesting. Put two stars next to those words and phrases.

7. Discuss students' word choices and emphasize how Cobb not only uses accurate and specific words, but also lively and engaging words to explore scientific information.

8. Arrange students into small groups and give each group a photocopied passage from *Blood & Gore* dealing with one of the following topics: Blood, Skin, Bone, Muscle, Nerves, Digestion, and Respiration.

9. Tell students to read their passage and think about how Cobb uses words to convey information about the human body.

10. Ask each group to make a poster advertising the importance of their assigned body part or function. Tell them their posters must include the following:

   ❋ a slogan that captures the importance of the body part or function

   ❋ text written in first person; they should write from the point of view of this body part or function

   ❋ information about what happens if their part or function is not working properly

   ❋ at least three fascinating facts about their part or function

   ❋ a picture (either drawn or photocopied) illustrating their part or function— where it fits into the body and how it works

11. If you wish, have students read and research more about their topics in books, magazines, or science-related Web sites.

12. Ask students to highlight words or phrases that specifically and accurately explain their topics so they stand out on their posters.

13. When the posters are finished, invite another class to your classroom and ask your students to share their posters. Invite the visiting students to vote for the poster that has the most specific and accurate use of scientific language.

| Lesson #4 | **CHOOSING WORDS THAT DEEPEN MEANING** |

New words are added to the English language regularly. Browse the latest edition of an unabridged dictionary in your school library. Chances are, you'll find words and phrases you never would have dreamed of finding just ten years ago, such as *9/11* and *blog*. In this lesson, students explore the dictionary and then come up with their own words and phrases to add to it and use in their writing.

MATERIALS:

   ❋ writing paper

   ❋ pens or pencils

   ❋ dictionaries

   ❋ drawing paper and markers

WHAT TO DO:

1. Encourage students to explore the dictionary and make lists on the board of words they find interesting.

2. Brainstorm a list of words students can't find in the dictionary but think should be added. These words might include slang or references to popular TV shows, commercials, movies, favorite foods, or music they enjoy, such as *Big Mac* or *fantabulous*.

3. Ask each student to select one word from the list and write it down.

4. Tell students to illustrate the word, putting it in an appropriate context to help a reader understand its meaning. For example, if the word is *Spider-Man*, the student might draw a picture of the superhero scaling the Empire State Building and casting a web.

5. Ask students to write one interesting thing about the word on the same page. They may write, for example, "Spider-Man is a brave hero who saves people."

6. Post the work in a place for everyone to read and enjoy. Encourage students to use the words in their writing.

Sentence Fluency Lessons

Read the final lines of E. B. White's *Charlotte's Web* (1952):

> Wilbur never forgot Charlotte. Although he loved her children and grandchildren dearly, none of the new spiders ever quite took her place in his heart. She was in a class by herself. It's not often that someone comes along who is a true friend and a good writer. Charlotte was both.

The first time we read this passage, we wondered, "Is this as well written as we think it is?" The second time confirmed it—"Yes!" The syntax, or the sentence structure, is masterful. Using short sentences followed by longer ones, and ending on the shortest one of all, creates a lovely cadence and nails the book's central message about the importance of communication and companionship.

The lessons that follow address the range of sentence fluency skills at play in every intermediate classroom, from crafting simple sentences to full-blown essays and stories. We've organized them into four key qualities:

❉ Capturing Smooth and Rhythmic Flow

❉ Crafting Well-Built Sentences

❉ Varying Sentence Patterns

❉ Breaking the "Rules" to Create Fluency

| Lesson #1 | **CAPTURING SMOOTH AND RHYTHMIC FLOW** |

In this lesson, we encourage you to read aloud "What Is Green?," one of many stunning poems in Mary O'Neill's *Hailstones and Halibut Bones* (1961). "What Is Green?" contains carefully chosen words in just the right places, producing smooth and rhythmic flow. Then discuss with students the importance of sentence fluency in both poetry and prose. From there, students try changing sentence beginnings and lengths in their own writing to create the same kind of flow they discovered in O'Neill's writing.

MATERIALS:

❋ a copy of *Hailstones and Halibut Bones* by Mary O'Neill

❋ chart paper with O'Neill's poem "What Is Green?" written on it

WHAT TO DO:

1. Discuss sentence fluency with students, emphasizing that it is the auditory trait. So when writers apply the trait, they think about the lengths of their sentences, the beginnings and endings of their sentences, how the words and phrases within their sentences sound, and how their sentences sound when they're strung together. Tell students that you will be reading aloud a poem and ask them to listen closely for fluency.

2. Read "What Is Green?" Take your time reading, emphasizing O'Neill's beautiful phrasing.

3. Enjoy yourself. When you're finished, ask students:

    ❋ "Did you think this piece was fluent?"

    ❋ "What did the writer do to make it sound good?"

    ❋ "What image or phrase stood out for you?"

    ❋ Show students the poem on the chart paper and ask: "Where is your favorite image or phrase? The beginning of a line? At the end? In the middle?"

4. Remind students that being fluent means writing sentences that do not all sound alike. Give them an example of a piece of writing with sentences that begin the same way and are the same length:

    ❋ My dog is big.   ❋ My dog is funny.

    ❋ My dog is red.   ❋ My dog smells.

5. Ask students to help you make one or more of these sentences more fluent. They might combine two or three sentences into one or they might try a new sentence beginning: "My big, red dog smells funny." "My dog is funny, and he smells." "It's funny to watch my big, red dog."

68

6. Write their revisions on the board or on a chart to illustrate how to make bland, boring sentences sound more interesting.

FOLLOW-UP ACTIVITY:

❋ Tell students that you are going to create a piece of writing together. Write the first sentence on the board or overhead, such as: "When I wake up in the morning, I'm excited to come to school," and then ask one of them to give you the next sentence. And here's the fun part: their new sentence must begin with the last word of the first sentence. For example; "School is a fun place to play and learn." (You can use a form of the word if it makes it easier for students, and for you!)

Lesson #2 CRAFTING WELL-BUILT SENTENCES

Most intermediate students struggle with sentence variety. They either write one long sentence or a series of short sentences, without understanding that the key to writing fluent pieces is *combining* sentences of differing lengths. What better way to build that understanding than by having children act out sentences? In this engaging lesson, students make sentences in a variety of lengths, using word cards, their bodies, and their imaginations.

> **MATERIALS:**
> ❋ 8½-by-11-inch cards
> ❋ markers

WHAT TO DO:

1. Come up with a basic sentence, such as "My dog is brown," and write each word on a separate card. Give the cards to four students and ask them to create the sentence by lining up in the right order with their cards facing out. Ask the students to read their sentence aloud one card at a time.

2. Create more cards with words for expanding the basic sentence. You could write "fuzzy" or "snuggly" to modify "dog." Give the cards to other students and ask them to figure out how to weave them into the basic sentence in a way that makes sense, then to stand where they think their word would go.

3. Add as many words as you like and allow students time to make the best sentence they can. Each time students incorporate a new word, have them read the sentence aloud in its entirety one card at a time.

4. Repeat this lesson often, using new, interesting words to help students learn how to write sentences of different lengths.

| Lesson #3 | **VARYING SENTENCE PATTERNS** |

*C*ome On, Rain! (1999) is an elegantly written book about a young girl and her mother who long for the rain on a hot summer's day. Because of its beautiful blend of dialogue and description, it invites expressive oral reading. Karen Hesse's words are pure poetry. This lesson uses *Come On, Rain!* as a model for showing students how to vary sentence length and type effectively in writing.

WHAT TO DO:

1. Tell students that you will be reading *Come On, Rain!* to them. But first, you want to review the different types of sentences that Karen Hesse uses in the book:

    Declarative: a statement
    Example: It was raining outside all day.

    Imperative: a command
    Example: Go get your boots and put them on.

    Interrogative: a question
    Example: Why aren't you wearing your rain boots?

    Exclamatory: an exclamation
    Example: Yikes!

> **MATERIALS:**
>
> ❖ a copy of *Come On, Rain!* by Karen Hesse
>
> ❖ photocopies of the Sentence Fluency Script (page 72)
>
> ❖ photocopies of the Sentence Fluency Cards (page 73)
>
> ❖ poster board
>
> ❖ markers

2. Write these definitions and examples on a transparency and offer other examples from *Come On, Rain!*

    ❖ Come on, rain! (exclamatory)

    ❖ I am sizzling like a hot potato. (declarative)

    ❖ Put on your suit and come straight over. (imperative)

    ❖ Is that thunder, Tessie? (interrogative)

    ❖ Slick with sweat, I run back home and slip up the steps past Mamma. (declarative)

    ❖ Stay where I can find you. (imperative)

    ❖ I hug Mamma hard, and she hugs me back. (declarative)

    ❖ May I put on my bathing suit? (interrogative)

3. Read *Come On, Rain!* slowly and carefully, emphasizing the finely crafted sentences throughout. Ask students to listen to how the sentences flow from beginning to end.

4. Ask for four volunteers to come to the front of the class. Give each one a copy of the Sentence Fluency Script (page 72), and assign parts. Tell the volunteers they will be reading the script aloud to the class and allow time for them to practice their lines.

5. While the volunteers are practicing, hand out photocopies of the Sentence Fluency Cards (page 73) to the rest of the class and have students cut them apart.

6. Ask the volunteers to read the script in its entirety, using expression to help the class begin to identify each type of sentence.

7. Have the volunteers read the script again, pausing after each line. Let the rest of the class determine which type of sentence was read and hold up the appropriate card. (Answers: 1. Declarative 2. Interrogative 3. Declarative 4. Interrogative 5. Declarative 6. Imperative 7. Declarative 8. Imperative 9. Exclamatory)

8. Inform students they are going to use these sentence types in a piece of their own about weather.

9. Brainstorm with the class different kinds of weather conditions such as snowy, foggy, hailing, sunny, and windy. Write the examples on the board.

10. Have students choose a partner and select one of the weather conditions as the subject for a piece of writing they will work on together: song lyrics to promote the positive qualities of the type of weather they chose.

11. Brainstorm with the class a list of familiar songs such as "Mary Had a Little Lamb," "Row, Row, Row Your Boat," The Hokey Pokey," "Old McDonald Had a Farm," and "B-I-N-G-O." Write these songs on the board and ask partners to pick one.

12. Tell partners to write out new lyrics for one verse of the song they chose, using as many of the sentence types as they can: declarative, imperative, interrogative, and exclamatory. Remind them that their song is going to be used to "sell" their type of weather, so they should include as much interesting information about it as possible.

13. When partners have completed a draft, ask them to assess their lyrics for sentence fluency and revise as necessary.

14. When students have finished revising their lyrics, ask them to put the new verse on a poster. Hang up the posters in a prominent place, and then sing all the songs as a class.

15. Ask students which songs contain the best sentence variety and vote for the song that best advertises a particular kind of weather. Discuss how sentence fluency makes the ideas more interesting.

16. Encourage students to write out their songs and send them to a local TV or radio station for use during an upcoming weather broadcast.

Sentence Fluency Script

Adapted from *Come On, Rain!* by Karen Hesse

READER 1: I hold my breath, waiting. A breeze blows the thin curtains into the kitchen, then sucks them back against the screen. (Declarative)

READER 2: "Is there thunder?" Mamma asks. (Interrogative)

READER 3: "No thunder," I say. (Declarative)

READER 4: "Is there lightning?" Mamma asks. (Interrogative)

READER 1: "No lightning," Jackie-Joyce says. (Declarative)

READER 2: "Stay where I can find you," Mamma says. (Imperative)

READER 3: "We will," I say. (Declarative)

READER 4: "Go on then," Mamma says, lifting the glass to her lips to take a sip. (Imperative)

ALL: "Come on, rain!" I cheer, peeling out of my clothes and into my suit, while Jackie-Joyce runs to get Liz and Rosemary. (Exclamatory)

 Getting Started With the Traits: Grades 3–5 © 2009 Ruth Culham and Raymond Coutu, Scholastic.

Sentence Fluency Cards

Interrogative

Declarative

Imperative

Exclamatory

BREAKING THE "RULES" TO CREATE FLUENCY

I n *One Tiny Turtle* (2001), Nicola Davies uses fluid, descriptive language to explain the life cycle of loggerhead sea turtles. And, as with her books on whales, bats, and polar bears, she drops in "factlets" throughout—interesting, well-researched bits of information that provide the reader with another way to interact with her beautifully written text. In this lesson, while listening to *One Tiny Turtle* read aloud, students determine whether sentences are complete or fragments. Then they use what they learn to write picture captions that present facts about loggerhead sea turtles.

> **MATERIALS:**
>
> ✴ a copy of *One Tiny Turtle* by Nicola Davies
>
> ✴ writing paper
>
> ✴ pens, pencils, markers, crayons
>
> ✴ chart paper

WHAT TO DO:

1. Ask students if they have ever heard of loggerhead sea turtles and, if so, to explain what they know.

2. Tell them you are going to read a book about loggerhead sea turtles and as you read, you'd like them to listen not only for fascinating pieces of information, but also for the author's sentence fluency—how she makes the text easy to listen to.

3. Read the book, pausing to show the pictures as you go. When you come to a page that has informational notes, or "factlets," show students how the author sets factlets apart from the running text. Ask if they hear any difference in the sentence fluency of factlets versus the running text.

4. Explain to students that complete sentences have a subject and a verb (a doer and an action). Fragments are only parts of sentences. Tell students that writers use complete sentences most often, but occasionally they use a fragment to change the way a passage sounds. Fragments can change the rhythm and tempo of the writing to make it pleasing to the ear. They can also be used to make important ideas stand out in the text.

5. Tell students you are going to reread some sentences from the book, and they are going to determine whether the sentences are complete or not by listening to them carefully.

6. Read the following sentences aloud to the students. Tell them to put a thumb up if they think a sentence is complete and down if they think it is not. If you wish, make an overhead to show after students have made their decisions.

   ✴ She's a baby, so her shell is soft as old leather. (thumb up)

   ✴ Safe in her world of weed (thumb down)

❋ Fish breathe underwater, but turtles are reptiles. (thumb up)

❋ She pokes her pinprick nostrils through the silver surface to take a quick breath, so fast, blink and you'd miss it! (thumb up)

❋ When you look for her (thumb down)

❋ Rides out the storm (thumb down)

❋ Her head is tough as a helmet. (thumb up)

❋ A glimpse of her (thumb down)

❋ Left behind, under the sand, her eggs stay deep and safe. (thumb up)

❋ And before the summer's over they wriggle from their shells. (thumb up)

❋ Swims and swims! (thumb down)

❋ One day, she'll remember this beach and come back. (thumb up)

7. Tell students they are going to try writing complete and incomplete sentences of their own. Ask them to recall a fact about loggerhead turtles from the text and write it out in a complete sentence.

8. Have students draw a picture to go along with their sentence and write a short caption underneath it that is a fragment.

9. Compare the two pieces of writing, pointing out for students what makes one a complete sentence and the other a fragment. Discuss how students can use fragments in their writing to change how the fluency sounds to the reader.

FOLLOW-UP ACTIVITIES:

❋ During the discussion of the book, students most likely had questions about loggerhead sea turtles that the book couldn't answer. Help them to write these questions out and use the Internet to find answers. Then, write the questions and answers on chart paper for all to see. Use complete sentences for the questions and fragments for the answers, explaining that writers do this all the time when they want to fit a lot of information into a small space.

❋ Read and enjoy other books by Nicola Davies, such as *Bat Loves the Night; Extreme Animals; White Owl, Barn Owl; Ice Bear; Big Blue Whale;* and *Surprising Sharks.* You and your students will delight in how beautifully Davies writes, and how fascinating she makes each animal.

Conventions Lessons

When it comes to teaching conventions, it's important to start simply and put students in control as quickly as possible. You can edit for students or you can teach them how to do it themselves. It's not a hard decision when put that way, is it? A word of warning, though: young writers won't edit as well, work as quickly, or be as thorough as mature writers. But if they learn new skills gradually, perhaps one each week, and practice until these skills become second nature, they will progress. Have faith in your students and in your teaching. The lessons that follow are called "warm-ups," quick reproducible activities designed to help you teach a range of skills, at the start of writing time:

* Checking Spelling

* Punctuating and Paragraphing Effectively

* Capitalizing Correctly

* Applying Grammar and Usage

To get to the point where students are truly in charge of their own editing, we have to abandon time-honored methods of correcting with a red pencil, giving students practice worksheets, and only publishing work that is perfect. These warm-ups will help you get your students to that point.

MATERIALS:

* overhead transparencies and photocopies of one of the Warm-Ups on pages 78–82, editor's marks on page 107

* a blank transparency

* photocopies of the Student-Friendly Scoring Guide for Conventions on page 112

WHAT TO DO:

1. Choose one of the Warm-Ups on pages 78–82. Make an overhead transparency of it, and the editor's marks on page 109. Also, make enough photocopies of both pages for each student in your class.

2. Project the Warm-Up transparency and briefly discuss the Check It! box at the bottom so students understand questions they should be asking themselves as they edit.

3. Distribute the photocopies of the Warm-Up and editor's marks. Tell students to complete the Warm-Up by themselves or with a partner, following the directions at the top of the sheet.

4. When they're finished, ask students to help you mark the errors on the Warm-Up transparency, using editor's marks. If you like, check their responses against the answer key on pages 83–84.

Lesson #2 **Warm-Up**

Use the editor's marks to correct the sentences below. The number of errors you should try to find is indicated after each sentence. Then use your corrected sentences to create a well-edited paragraph on a separate sheet.

Lesson #1 **Warm-Up**

Use the editor's marks to correct the sentences below. The number of errors you should try to find is indicated after each sentence. Then use your corrected sentences to create a well-edited paragraph on a separate sheet of paper.

A individual from History I realy admire is abraham lincoln (6)

he is an intresting person and a Great president, to. (5)

It musta been very hard back in the 1860S to fight aganst all the people which wanted to kepe slavery. (6)

But if lincoln hadnt be strong and stood up for his beleifs, we wood not have abolished slavery. (5)

he was the rite man to be President of the united states' at the time. (6)

Check It!

Is the punctuation correct and does it guide the reader through the text?
Did I capitalize all the right words?
Is my spelling accurate—especially for words I read and write a lot?
Did I follow grammar rules to make my writing clear and readable?
Did I indent paragraphs in all the right places?

See answers, page 83, and editor's marks, page 109.

78

5. From there, have students share the well-edited paragraphs they created on a separate sheet of paper. Write a well-edited paragraph of your own on a blank transparency.

6. If time allows, encourage students to choose pieces from their writing folders to edit for spelling, punctuation, capitalization, and grammar and usage. Then have them assess their work using the Student-Friendly Scoring Guide on page 112. Linking Warm-Ups to their own work builds independence.

For scores of reproducible warm-ups to share with your students, see *Daily Trait Warm-Ups: 180 Revision and Editing Activities to Kick Off Writing Time* (Scholastic, 2009).

Warm-Up

Use the editor's marks to correct the sentences below. The number of errors you should try to find is indicated after each sentence. Then use your corrected sentences to create a well-edited paragraph on a separate sheet of paper.

A individual from History I realy admire is abraham lincoln (6)

he is an intresting person and a Great president, to. (5)

It musta been very hard back in the 1860S to fight aganst all the people which wanted to kepe slavery. (6)

But if lincoln hadnt be strong and stood up for his beleifs, we wood not have abolished slavery. (5)

he was the rite man to be President of the united states' at the time. (6)

Check It!

❉ Is the punctuation correct and does it guide the reader through the text?

❉ Did I capitalize all the right words?

❉ Is my spelling accurate—especially for words I read and write a lot?

❉ Did I follow grammar rules to make my writing clear and readable?

❉ Did I indent paragraphs in all the right places?

See answers, page 83, and editor's marks, page 109.

Warm-Up

Use the editor's marks to correct the sentences below. The number of errors you should try to find is indicated after each sentence. Then use your corrected sentences to create a well-edited paragraph on a separate sheet of paper.

Skatebording can be an Art a Hobby a Sport, or just a way to get around conveniently. (6)

some peopl call it a extreem sport because it is so creativ. (5)

In 2002, a report from the marketing research firm american sports' data revealed that their were 12.5 million skateboarders in the world. (5)

Eigty percent of those Skateboarder's were under the age of 18, & 74 percent is mail. (6)

Skate Boarding are a sport that has really taken of in the last 20 yeers. (5)

Check It!

❊ Is the punctuation correct and does it guide the reader through the text?

❊ Did I capitalize all the right words?

❊ Is my spelling accurate—especially for words I read and write a lot?

❊ Did I follow grammar rules to make my writing clear and readable?

❊ Did I indent paragraphs in all the right places?

See answers, page 83, and editor's marks, page 109.

Warm-Up

Use the editor's marks to correct the sentences below. The number of errors you should try to find is indicated after each sentence. Then use your corrected sentences to create a well-edited paragraph on a separate sheet of paper.

Becomeing a Teacher is alot of hard work and takes meny year's of Study. (6)

They are a wonder ful job, however, 'cuz you get to help kids' lern. (6)

what culd possibly be moore rewarding then that (5)

Although their are many difficult things to learn to be a good Teacher, its a very worthwhile Profesion. (5)

helping a New Generation learn how to read & rite is an awesome responsibility and alot of fun, to. (7)

Check It!

✱ Is the punctuation correct and does it guide the reader through the text?

✱ Did I capitalize all the right words?

✱ Is my spelling accurate—especially for words I read and write a lot?

✱ Did I follow grammar rules to make my writing clear and readable?

✱ Did I indent paragraphs in all the right places?

See answers, page 83, and editor's marks, page 109.

Getting Started With the Traits: Grades 3–5 © 2009 Ruth Culham and Raymond Coutu, Scholastic.

Warm-Up

Use the editor's marks to correct the sentences below. The number of errors you should try to find is indicated after each sentence. Then use your corrected sentences to create a well-edited paragraph on a separate sheet of paper.

last year there was two earthquakes you could really feel in san Francisco. (3)

I know because my friends cusin lives their. (3)

She calls california the shaek-n-bake state because they are so many earthquakes and it was so hot. (4)

buildings has to be bilt to a special code to make sure their stable. (4)

Otherwise, theyl just crumbled into dust (3)

Check It!

❊ Is the punctuation correct and does it guide the reader through the text?

❊ Did I capitalize all the right words?

❊ Is my spelling accurate—especially for words I read and write a lot?

❊ Did I follow grammar rules to make my writing clear and readable?

❊ Did I indent paragraphs in all the right places?

See answers, page 84, and editor's marks, page 109.

Warm-Up

Use the editor's marks to correct the sentences below. The number of errors you should try to find is indicated after each sentence. Then use your corrected sentences to create a well-edited paragraph on a separate sheet of paper.

Its so hard togo to bed wen my parents tell me too (5)

i try hard to fall asleep, but its not easy when its still light out or when im not tyred. (5)

Sometimes I hid a book under the covers and read latee in to the nyght (5)

I turns the light out really fast if I here my Mom or dad comming to chek on me (6)

with the covers puled up, I try to breathe normaly until them have left the room, and than I go back to reading untill I fall asleep. (6)

Check It!

❋ Is the punctuation correct and does it guide the reader through the text?

❋ Did I capitalize all the right words?

❋ Is my spelling accurate—especially for words I read and write a lot?

❋ Did I follow grammar rules to make my writing clear and readable?

❋ Did I indent paragraphs in all the right places?

See answers, page 84, and editor's marks, page 109.

 Getting Started With the Traits: Grades 3–5 © 2009 Ruth Culham and Raymond Coutu, Scholastic.

Answer Key

LESSON #1

An individual from History I really admire is abraham lincoln. he is an intresting person and a Great president, to. It musta been very hard back in the 1860$ to fight aganst all the peopl which wanted to kepe slavery. But if lincoln hadnt be strong and stood up for his beleifs we wood not have abolished slavery. he was the rite man to be President of the united states at the time.

An individual from history I really admire is Abraham Lincoln. He was an interesting person and a great president, too. It must have been very hard back in the 1860s to fight against all the people who wanted to keep slavery. But if Lincoln hadn't been strong and stood up for his beliefs, we would not have abolished slavery. He was the right man to be president of the United States at the time.

LESSON #2

Skatebording can be an Art a Hobby, a Sport, or just a way to get around conveniently. some peopl call it a extreem sport because it is so creativ. In 2002, a report from the marketing research firm american sports data revealed that their were 12.5 million skateboarders in the world. Eigty percent of those Skateboarders were under the age of 18, & 74 percent is mail. Skate Boarding are a sport that has really taken of in the last 20 yeers.

Skateboarding can be an art, a hobby, a sport, or just a way to get around conveniently. Some people call it an extreme sport because it is so creative. In 2002, a report from the marketing research firm American Sports Data revealed that there were 12.5 million skateboarders in the world. Eighty percent of those skateboarders were under the age of 18, and 74 percent were male. Skateboarding is a sport that has really taken off in the last 20 years.

LESSON #3

Becomeing a Teacher is alot of hard work and takes meny years of Study. They are a wonderful job, however, cuz you get to help kids lern. what culd possibly be moore rewarding then that? Although their are many difficult things to learn to be a good Teacher, it's a very worthwhile Profesion. helping a New Generation learn how to read & rite is an awesome responsibility and alot of fun, to.

Becoming a teacher is a lot of hard work and takes many years of study. It is a wonderful job, however, because you get to help kids learn. What could possibly be more rewarding than that? Although there are many difficult things to learn to be a good teacher, it's a very worthwhile profession. Helping a new generation learn how to read and write is an awesome responsibility and a lot of fun, too.

LESSON #4

last year there **were** ~~was~~ two earthquakes you could really feel in san Francisco.

I know because my friends (cusin) lives (their.)

She calls california the (shaek)-n-bake state because they are so many earthquakes and it **is** ~~was~~ so hot.

buildings **have** ~~has~~ to be (bilt) to a special code to make sure (their) stable.

Otherwise, (theyl) just crumbled into dust ⊙

Last year there were two earthquakes you could really feel in San Francisco. I know because my friend's cousin lives there. She calls California the shake-n-bake state because there are so many earthquakes and it is so hot. Buildings have to be built to a special code to make sure they're stable. Otherwise, they'll just crumble into dust.

LESSON #5

Its so hard to go to bed (wen) my parents tell me (too) ⊙

i try hard to fall asleep, but its not easy when its still light out or when im not (tyred)

Sometimes I **hide** ~~hid~~ a book under the covers and read late in to the (nyght) ⊙

I turns the light out really fast if I (here) my Mom or dad (comming) to (chek) on me ⊙

with the covers (puled) up, I try to breathe (normaly) until (them) have left the room, and (than) I go back to reading untill I fall asleep.

It's so hard to go to bed when my parents tell me to. I try hard to fall asleep but it's not easy when it's still light out or when I'm not tired. Sometimes I hide a book under the covers and read late into the night. I turn the light out really fast if I hear my mom or dad coming to check on me. With the covers pulled up, I try to breathe normally until they have left the room, and then I go back to reading until I fall asleep.

Publishing Tips

After students have gotten what they want to say down on paper, they are ready to publish. Publishing is an important step because, finally, it makes the writing available to the audience for which it is intended. Student writing may be put on bulletin boards, made into books, shared with other classes or audiences, or sent home as "finished." When students are ready to have their work go public, consider these tips.

* Keep available plenty of writing supplies such as pens, pencils, markers, and paper of different types and colors, as well as scissors, tape, glue, and stickers. Take time to show students how to make books by folding paper and, if they are ready, cutting and stapling the books. Keep models available for students to follow.

* Encourage students to practice making neat letters in their own writing, not on worksheets. Ask students to select a sentence or passage to rewrite in their best handwriting.

* Remind students to leave plenty of space between lines in drafts to allow room for revisions and edits.

* Show students interesting text layouts as you discover them. One of our favorites is the Geronimo Stilton chapter-book series from Scholastic. Key words and phrases throughout the texts are presented in color and creative shapes for emphasis. Encourage students to try writing this way.

* Hang students' work in the room, in the hallway, and all around the school.

* Attach a photo of the student to his or her work to make a powerful connection between the writing and the writer. If possible, add a photo of a parent or guardian with the child to reinforce the fact that writing should extend beyond school walls.

* Help students keep writer's notebooks all year. At the end of the year, collect them, gift-wrap them over the summer, and return them to students at the start of the following school year. After clearing their minds over the summer and then reading their entries from the year before, chances are students will be amazed by their progress in all traits and be excited to dive back in.

Concluding Thought

You know better than anyone that working with upper-elementary students can be messy. Holding their attention, keeping them on task, and moving them forward is a challenge. But with the right routines in place, it's not impossible. In fact, it can be extremely satisfying for you and your students. Carrying out whole-class lessons on a regular basis is an essential routine. Another one is providing practice opportunities through independent and small-group work. In the next chapter, you'll find a host of activities that are perfect for doing just that.

Trait-Based Activities for Independent and Small-Group Work

Once you've had a chance to work on a trait as a whole group, it's important to give students a chance to practice the trait on their own. This chapter contains activities designed to get them started. You'll find eight activities for each trait, organized by key quality—fun, classroom-tested activities that are sure to get your students drafting, revising, editing, and sharing their finished work with great pride.

We've also included student-friendly scoring guides for each trait (pages 110–112), so students can easily assess their work as they write and look for places to revise and edit. These scoring guides can be used in conjunction with the revision checklist (page 108) and the list of editor's marks (page 109), which contain handy reminders of things all writers need to think about as they bring their work to completion.

Ideas Activities

FINDING A TOPIC

Free Ideas

The topics we enjoy writing about most are the ones that matter to us. So help students look for experiences and ideas they really care about. Here are some ways to do that:

❋ *Free writing:* Ask students, "What's on your mind? What have you been thinking about lately? What are you feeling right now?" Then suggest they "Start writing to find out! One idea will lead to others."

❋ *Flashback:* Have students look through their journal entries or family photographs for ideas. Or have them dig out old toys, collections, or souvenirs at home. Encourage them to look for things that stimulate memories and feelings.

❋ *Favorite places:* Invite students to think about some place they love to go: the beach, the mountains, their grandparents' house, a tree house, a playing field, or an amusement park. Make a class list of favorite places to go and things to do there. From there, start writing.

Corral Ideas

Jotting down interesting tidbits as we encounter them is a good way to find ideas. And a writer's notebook is an excellent tool for doing that. As students ask questions about something the class is reading, something they heard on the news, or as you help them make the links between what they are studying and what they still want to know, have them write these kernels of ideas down in a notebook. These kernels can be big or small, old or new. Students just need a place to capture what intrigues them, issues that cause them to question things, and observations they make that fascinate them. Then later, when it is time to write, they can look back in their notebook and find things they have probably forgotten, but may make for interesting ideas for study, research, and writing. With notebooks, you may never hear "I don't know what to write about" again!

FOCUSING THE TOPIC

Call It Out

Pick a category such as "animals." Call out questions and encourage students to chime in with different answers. Go from general questions to narrow ones, such as "What kind of animal is it? Where does it live? What does it eat? Does it do anything interesting? What is a predator of this animal?" It should only take three to five minutes to work through a whole cycle, from a general topic to a narrow one. Keep asking questions until the category has been examined from many possible views. Then record some of the narrowed topics on the board and let students do a quick write, about five minutes long, on one of them.

Picture This

Bring in a poster-sized art print of a complex and interesting work that you think your students will enjoy analyzing, such as Pablo Picasso's *Guernica*. Display the print and ask students to write down what they see in a series of statements (complete or not). Next, take six precut pieces of paper, which together would cover the entire picture, and cover five-sixths of the print. Now, ask students to look closely at what they see and describe it. Continue moving the paper so that students get a chance to describe all six parts of the poster out of context. Finally, uncover the whole picture again and ask them to describe it one more time. Not only will they be more focused and use better descriptions, but they will also create a richer variety of work as a class.

DEVELOPING THE TOPIC

Ask Me a Question

Divide students into groups of three. Each student tells the group a short story of a memorable event in his or her life. The listeners cannot comment during or after. Instead, they write on a piece of paper three questions for the storyteller. They hand questions to the storyteller. That way, the storyteller becomes aware of details he or she might have left out, which can be included next time the story is told, either orally or in writing.

Leave It Out

Rewrite a familiar story—a simple story your students have read and enjoyed, such as "Rumpelstiltskin." Take out some of the juicy details, ones that are important to the central idea of the story, such as the guessing of the name or the wishes. Share the story as you rewrote it and ask students what is missing. Now read the original. Discuss which version makes more sense, is more interesting, and why. Help students discover that taking time to elaborate and fill in the blanks for the reader is an important step in making their ideas clear.

USING DETAILS

Observe Closely, Then Write

Ask students to observe their surroundings while hiking in the park, having a snack in the playground, or enjoying a day at the beach, and record their observations on a chart. (See example at right.) Be sure they sit long enough to observe details—small creatures scurrying by or clouds high above, for instance. Make students dig deep and use their senses. Ask them to report to their classmates things that were most interesting, important, and unusual. As a final step, students can write longer pieces about their experiences. Encourage them to show, not just tell. Teach them how to expand their ideas by including lively details. Compile these writings into a book.

Name MATT K.	Date	Location Forest Park	
What I:	Interesting	Important	Unusual
Saw SMALL YOUNG BUSHES DIFFERENT SIZES. GROWING IN THE OPEN BURNED SPACES. LOTS OF BEETLE-T. TREES	BIG DEAD TREES, BURNED SCARRED TRUNKS		
Heard AT LEAST 3 DIFFERENT KINDS OF BIRDS - SOME ALL THE TIME, SOME JUST A FEW CHIRPS			BIG TRUCKS, MAYBE LOGGING OVER THE HILLS OUT OF SIGHT- CONSTANT DRONING
Felt UNEVEN FOREST FLOOR UNDER MY SHOES, MAKES IT	SUNSHINE ON MY FACE WARM HARD TO WALK FAST. DEAD CRUMBY PINE NEEDLES.		
Smelled	DEEP BREATHES, FEELS GOOD, NO POLLUTION, CRISP, FRESH		
Tasted			PB&J SANDWICH Really TASTES GOOD THE WALK MADE ME HUNGRY, BUT FOOD TASTES BETTER THAN USUAL.

Pick the Postcard

Find a set of postcards on a single topic such as dogs, beach scenes, or city buildings. (You'll find them at most stores that sell greeting cards, as well as museum stores and stationery stores.) Give one postcard to each student and ask them to write a paragraph about the image that is so descriptive, readers will be able to identify the postcard in the set. Once students have finished writing, collect and display all the postcards. Have students read their paragraphs aloud and see if classmates can guess the card. Discuss the techniques that some writers used that made the matching of the text to the card easier—the more specific the details, the quicker the match.

Organization Activities

CREATING THE LEAD

Share Student Leads

Ask students to share just the leads from their work. As they read them in small groups or in a large circle, their classmates get ideas of different ways to begin their work.

After everyone has read, brainstorm a general list of different techniques to begin writing, and then identify those techniques a writer would use for specific kinds of writing. Encourage students to try several different leads before settling on the final one.

Share Examples From Literature

Share short excerpts from a variety of different sources so students can see how professional writers choose to begin their work. Here are some examples of beginnings that work tremendously well:

"What they don't understand about birthdays and what they never tell you is that when you're eleven, you're also ten, and nine, and eight, and seven, and six, and five and four, and three, and two and one."
—Sandra Cisneros, *Woman Hollering Creek*, from "Eleven," 1991

"Gramps says that I am a country girl at heart, and that is true. I have lived most of my thirteen years in Bybanks, Kentucky, which is not much more than a caboodle of houses rooting in a green spot alongside the Ohio River."
—Sharon Creech, *Walk Two Moons*, 1994

> ### WAYS TO BEGIN A PIECE OF WRITING
>
> ❋ A thought-provoking question to make the reader wonder
>
> ❋ A little "sip" of the conclusion to get the reader's attention and pique his or her interest
>
> ❋ A funny story or personal anecdote to set a humorous or individual tone
>
> ❋ A list of main points to introduce the topic in a serious, logical, and straightforward manner
>
> ❋ A dramatic, sweeping, or eye-opening statement
>
> ❋ An expert quotation to establish credibility from the start
>
> ❋ The student's own angle—one that readers have never seen before

"It was not that Omri didn't appreciate Patrick's birthday present to him. Far from it. He was really very grateful—sort of. It was, without a doubt, very kind of Patrick to give Omri anything at all, let alone a secondhand plastic Indian that he himself had finished with."
—Lynne Reid Banks *The Indian in the Cupboard*, 1980

USING SEQUENCE WORDS

Mix It Up

To reinforce sequencing, reorder a poem, magazine article, literature story, recipe, student paper, or any other kind of continuous text and ask students to reassemble it in the correct order. Cut the text into pieces so students can play with it like a puzzle. Ask them to look for transition words, the lead sentence, then the conclusion. It is important to start with a concrete, linear piece of writing and then move on to pieces that are more abstract.

Putting It in Order

Read aloud a familiar story to a group. When you're finished, choose a child to stand and tell the beginning of the story. Then choose another child to stand and tell the ending. Next, have another child tell the middle of the story, while standing between the children who told the beginning and ending. Have more volunteers add to the story, placing them in their logical position in line.

STRUCTURING THE BODY

Teach Organizational Options

Information can be organized in many ways. Helping students choose the best way is a little like picking out shoes. Sometimes they might want dressy and formal; other times, more relaxed and casual. Maybe one of these organizational "shoes" fits their topic and purpose— or perhaps they can find another style or structure that's a better fit. It's our job to help students try things on, to guide them.

❋ **Organizing by Space.** If students were describing, say, a room, they might begin with the big impression—size or color—then move gradually to smaller details: furniture, windows, lighting, rugs; then toys, pictures, figurines; then the spider on the window ledge, the half-eaten candy bar, the open book, the sock on the rug.

❋ **Organizing by Time.** If students are writing stories, or explaining events, they might organize chronologically. Be sure they include specific events, but not every one, because their papers will grow too big, sprawling, and unmanageable. This can happen if students begin too far before the real story even starts. They shouldn't keep going too long after the real story ends, either. Encourage students to keep their stories small—begin with what matters, and when the story ends, stop.

❖ **Organizing by Content.** Let's say a student is writing an informational piece on black bears. The student could begin by listing all the important things he or she knows. For the body of the paper, he or she might group details together into subcategories; for example, what black bears eat, where they live, their natural enemies, and so on. From there, the student would write paragraphs developing these categories. This approach keeps a writer from skipping around. Then, encourage the student to end with a surprise or an important tidbit: "Though often feared, black bears rarely attack people." Discourage him or her from "pre-organizing" the writing into nice, little five-paragraph themes. If there are more than five subcategories, great. If there are fewer, but with more details, that's fine, too.

❖ **Organizing by Perspective.** For a persuasive essay, it is important to keep everything focused on the main issue. Have students begin with a clear statement of their position. Then, tell them to lay out the arguments in favor of and against the issue. Students should give the best evidence they can to support the side they feel is right. Urge them to end with a strong conclusion that focuses on the advantages of their position.

ENDING WITH A SENSE OF RESOLUTION

Look to Authors

Probably the best way to study endings is to read a bunch of them. There are so many pieces of fiction and nonfiction available—pieces that you and your students will enjoy reading as you observe how the writers crafted their conclusions. Select a few models from literature that show the variety of techniques authors use. Here are a few to get you started:

A Profound Thought—to take a bit of common knowledge to a new level
> Example: "Miss Honey was still hugging the tiny girl in her arms and neither of them said a word as they stood there watching the big black car tearing round the corner at the end of the road and disappearing forever into the distance."
> —Roald Dahl, *Matilda*, 1988

A Surprise—to close on an unexpected note, inspired by an important moment or recurring theme in the text
> Example: "Once again, the tarot cards lay before him. Once again, he heard the cathedral bells ring twelve times. At the stroke of midnight, he flipped over the first card. It was THE SERVANT. Smiling broadly, Fabrizio turned the next card. . . ."
> —Avi, *Midnight Magic*, 1999

A Quote—to reinforce key points made in the text

> Example: "Very softly, she half sang, half hummed a song that her grandmother used to sing . . . 'If only, if only, the moon speaks no reply; Reflecting the sun and all that's gone by. Be strong my weary wolf, turn around boldly, Fly high, my baby bird, My angel, my only.'"
> —Louis Sachar, *Holes*, 1998

A Tie-Up—to take care of loose ends and answer lingering questions the reader may still have about key points

> Example: "Then I ran ahead to put the plates on the table."
> —Jean Fritz, *Homesick: My Own Story*, 1982

A Question or Open-Ended Statement—to leave the reader on an uncertain note

> Example: "And soon, they were rolling on again, leaving Treegap behind, and as they went, the tinkling little melody of a music box drifted out behind them and was lost at last far down the road."
> —Natalie Babbitt, *Tuck Everlasting*, 1975

A Challenge—to take action

> Example: "Be smarter than I was: Go talk to Grandma and Grandpa, Mom and Dad and other relatives and friends. Discover and remember what they have to say about what they learned growing up. By keeping their stories alive you make them, and yourself, immortal."
> —Christopher Paul Curtis, *Bud, Not Buddy*, 1999

A Summary—to make key points one more time

> Example: "And because so many of them were always begging him to tell and tell again the story of his adventures on the peach, he thought it would be nice if one day he sat down and wrote a book. So he did. And that is what you have just finished reading."
> —Roald Dahl, *James and the Giant Peach*, 1961

A Literary Device—to create a lasting image using, for example, a metaphor

> Example: "This is why, walking across a school campus on this particular December morning, I keep searching the sky. As if I expected to see, rather like hearts, a lost pair of kites hurrying toward heaven."
> —Truman Capote, *A Christmas Memory*, 1956

A Laugh—to make the reader smile at the end

> Example: "'Oh, I will,' said Harry, and they were surprised at the grin that was spreading over his face. 'They don't know we're not allowed to use magic at home. I'm going to have a lot of fun with Dudley this summer. . . .'"
> —J. K. Rowling, *Harry Potter and the Sorcerer's Stone*, 1997

Practice What You See

Ask students to choose one of the techniques and try it on a piece of their own writing to see if it works. Have them share their endings in small groups and offer suggestions for revisions to one another. Don't forget to include picture books as resources. Since picture books are so short, you can examine many different techniques rather quickly. Another good way to look for well-crafted endings is to read through nonfiction sources such as encyclopedias, research articles, letters, and memos.

Voice Activities

ESTABLISHING A TONE

Illustrate the Trait

Students will enjoy the challenge of drawing visual representations of voice (or any of the traits, for that matter). They can write out their own explanation of the trait, or draw a picture or icon they feel represents the trait. Creating a visual representation of the trait enables students to think deeply about the central meaning of the trait.

Voice Out, Voice In

This is a simple activity, but it works well. Find a sample of writing that is devoid of voice. They are everywhere. Manuals and textbooks are often a good source; memos are, too. Have students, working individually or in pairs, rewrite the piece, trying to put in as much voice as possible. Read the revisions aloud to appreciate the contrast.

Try this activity in reverse, too. Strange as it may seem, taking voice out of a piece is also a good activity for building students' awareness of this trait, since to remove it, they must understand what it is!

CONVEYING THE PURPOSE

Voice in Art

Gather four or five art prints that depict the same subject, such as fruit, people, scenery, or buildings. Make sure you choose artists whose styles differ significantly. Your school's media center may have study prints, or your local art museum may have pictures that it loans to schools for art education programs. Don't forget the Internet. Images of art through the centuries, from old-world to modern, are readily available online.

Ask students to compare the prints and make lists of the ways they are alike and how they are different. If you choose images of people, for instance, ask students to give you specific examples of how a picture of a man by Picasso is different from one by Michelangelo. Help students see that each artist develops a distinctive voice through his or her work and, over time, that voice becomes recognizable to others.

Compare and Contrast

Find two or three books on the same topic, but by authors with different styles. For young children, a good place to begin is with folk or fairy tales—two versions of "Cinderella," for instance. There are wonderful examples of fairy tales that have been written in traditional narrative form and also as scripts for plays.

Older students might like to look at the differences in an expository text on the same topic. Find an encyclopedia entry on, say, spiders. Now look in other places, such as a museum guide that accompanies an exhibit on spiders, or a science magazine such as *Ranger Rick*, to find other examples of writing about the creature. Where else might you go? How about an excerpt from a novel such as *Spider Boy* (1997) by Ralph Fletcher? Now look at the different ways the author of each piece writes about spiders. Trust us, there will be a significant difference in voice.

CREATING A CONNECTION TO THE AUDIENCE

Make a Book of Books You Love

The books we love most are often those that ring with voice. Make lists of favorites and share them aloud. Keep a class book of favorites and ask students to add names and titles to it regularly. And be sure to tell students what you've been reading. Share favorite passages and let them see how good writing affects you. Give students time to do the same, either in small groups, in large groups, or with younger students. Listen carefully to what they have to say. What a refreshing alternative to the standard book report. And, look, no papers to correct!

New Voices, New Choices

Have students write the first sentence of a letter to five different audiences. If students are studying the effects of global warming, for instance, ask them to write to the local newspaper, their grandmother, an anti-environmentalist, a friend, and the president of a local consumer-rights group. Discuss how the voice in the writing will change depending on the intended audience. Students can also share other places to which they might write letters and who the audience would be. Now ask them to describe the voice that would be appropriate for each of those audiences.

TAKING RISKS TO CREATE VOICE

Historically BOLD?

Think back to the people and events that really stick in your mind. What makes this person or event so memorable? Talk to students about it. If the event changed history, or if the person accomplished something extraordinary, point out that history is determined by people who are bold and willing to stand up for what they believe in. This is what we want students to do in their writing, after all: take a stand, defend a position, think about things in new ways, astound and amaze us. Voice will help them do that.

You can extend this activity, too. After the discussion, ask students to assume the point of view of an important historical figure, such as Albert Einstein, Rosa Parks, or Sacagawea, and write a letter of application for a job. Brainstorm with the students what kinds of jobs each person might want to pursue. In their letters, encourage students to assume the powerful voice of this person in such a way that he or she would surely get the job.

The Old Switcheroo

Ask students to think about a favorite story, such as "Goldilocks and the Three Bears" or "Cinderella." Allow time for them to tell the story to a partner. Next, challenge students to change their story by telling it from the point of view of one of the other characters, or from someone who might have a different perspective on the event. After students have told and retold their stories, ask them if the voice changed. If so, why? If not, why not?

Word Choice Activities

APPLYING STRONG VERBS

Active and Passive Verbs

Nothing works harder in a sentence than the verb. Pound for pound, students get their money's worth by paying attention to the power that verbs bring to the piece. Other word forms carry a great deal of impact, such as precise nouns and modifiers. But in our book, it's the verbs that earn the most respect. And the use of active verbs over passive verbs makes the writing more vigorous. Consider the following:

While running, Frankie passed Johnny. (*active voice*)
While running, Johnny was passed by Frankie. (*passive voice*)

Ask students to find an example of each in one of their textbooks, and give them this advice: If the subject is the doer, the verb is in the active voice. If the subject is the receiver, the verb is in the passive voice.

Here's to Adverbs—or Not!

Want to have some fun with parts of speech? Try this. Divide the class into an even number of groups: pros and cons. Review the list of parts of speech students should know, and ask a set of two groups to debate the pros and cons—to use it or not, how to use it well in writing, how to abuse it. Make sure there is a pro and a con to each part of speech—one group that's for using it, another that's against using it. Use these jewels of examples from Mem Fox and Stephen King to get students started.

> Pro: "In the same way that weak nouns require adjectives to pep them up, weak verbs scream out for adverbs to help them along."
> —Mem Fox, (1993)

> Con: "I believe the road to hell is paved with adverbs . . . they're like dandelions. If you have one on your lawn, it looks pretty and unique. If you fail to root it out, however, you find five the next day . . . fifty the day after that. . . ."
> —Stephen King, (2000)

SELECTING STRIKING WORDS AND PHRASES

Rice Cakes or Salsa?

As students discover some of the less interesting words in their work, teach them to ask, "Is this a 'rice cake' word or a 'salsa' word?" Every paper should have salsa words! Use this analogy frequently, and students will begin to use it every day. One teacher shared that at the end of the day, as she was dismissing class, she said, "Have a nice afternoon and evening." To which a few students replied, "*Nice* is a rice cake word!"

Words, Words Everywhere

One year Ruth was assigned to a classroom that had no windows. It was truly awful. The students and she missed seeing the first snow, the brilliant blue sky, the bursts of rain that would soak them to the skin in just a minute or two—all the beauty of the outside world. During these long, sensory-deprived years in the classroom, she discovered a way to help students with words.

1. On 4- x 6-inch strips of bright neon paper that doesn't fade over time (you can buy it at an office supply store), print in bold the words you are discovering during reading and writing activities. Be sure to include precise nouns, descriptive adjectives, and energetic verbs.

2. Write each word on a slip of paper that is color coded according to part of speech: for example, red for verbs, green for nouns, and blue for adjectives. With the help of the students, pin the slips to the ceiling.

3. As you read and find new words to add throughout the year, have students look them up and write them on the color-coded slips of paper. Not only will they get practice spotting new and interesting words, determining their parts of speech, and building a collection, they will use the words in their writing.

4. Everyone needs to tune out and daydream occasionally, and since Ruth's students had no window to gaze out, she gave them words to stare at. She was surprised at how many of those words found their way into student writing. They were bright, colorful, and useful. It helped.

USING SPECIFIC AND ACCURATE WORDS

The More Detail, the Better

Have all students study the same object to see who can observe the most details—and the most *unusual* details. If possible, use a live (and lively!) subject for this activity—a chameleon or tarantula, for instance. Give students one minute to study the object you have selected, then put it away. Now allow one minute for students to write down everything they can remember about the object. Share ideas as a group and make one big list of details for the object. Repeat this activity several times until students begin seeing details easily and are able to record quite a few in the time allowed.

Describe It, Then Build It

Create two identical collections of building materials—blocks, sticks, cardboard, paper, pipe cleaners, corks, buttons, paper clips, and so forth. Then have students work in teams of three. One student builds something from the collection while a second student waits in another room or behind a barrier with the same collection of building materials. The third student observes the first construction, then describes it in detail to the second builder, who tries to replicate the creation of the first builder. The second builder must work only from the description without looking at the first builder's creation. After about fifteen minutes, tell the teams to stop and get together to observe their constructions. As a class, discuss the role of specific and accurate details, particularly when giving directions or instructions.

CHOOSING WORDS THAT DEEPEN MEANING

Is More Always Better?

If your students have discovered descriptive language and are trying just a little too hard to make sure every sentence is chock full of it, you might show them the other side of the coin. We want students to try new ways of saying things—even if, at first, it isn't very successful. But we don't want them to think that more is necessarily better all the time. Try rewriting common signs such as road signs, warning signs, business signs, and so forth, using flowery and highly descriptive language. Compare the original to the rewrite and challenge students to be specific about why one is more effective than the other. For example: "Caution: Children Crossing" could be overwritten to: "You better slow down a little. There are some pretty nice kids who go to school here and they often walk or ride their bikes along here. Sometimes they aren't listening and looking for traffic, and it could be dangerous for them if you didn't slow down." That would be quite a road sign, wouldn't it? Sometimes one or two words work more effectively than longer, more descriptive sentences.

What's in a Word?

Choose a word that everyone uses when things are going well or to describe a good situation, such as *cool*. Ask students to write a list of other everyday words and phrases that mean the same thing—things they might hear in conversation or find in stories. Also, have students go home and interview one or two people from an earlier generation for more synonyms for *cool*. Gather as many examples as possible as a class. Here are some starters to seed the list if necessary:

bad	*outta sight*	*terrific*
super-duper	*rad*	*hip*
awesome	*groovy*	*happenin'*
fantabulous	*excellent*	*hot*
tight	*far out*	*phat*

Sort the words into three categories: (1) the way I say it, (2) the way my parents say it, and (3) the way my grandparents say it. Make a chart to hang in the room. As students hear new ways to express the idea, invite them to add those words to the list. By examining contemporary language use, students find that every generation develops its own way to express itself, even when the expressions themselves wind up being similar. Cool, dude.

Sentence Fluency Activities

CAPTURING SMOOTH AND RHYTHMIC FLOW

I've Got Rhythm

Hearing good language read aloud builds fluency even in young writers who are themselves not yet ready to begin writing complex sentences. Share a piece of poetry that's fun to read aloud. Some poems work so hard at rhyming that much of the natural flow is lost, so pick one that is easy to read aloud and emphasizes the use of comfortable, natural language. Some prose pieces, such as Mem Fox's *Tough Boris* (1994) and *Koala Lou* (1989), also have natural rhythm and repeating refrains that students pick up and repeat on their own.

Music to Our Ears

Use the music of classic works such as "Peter and the Wolf" and "Carnival of the Animals" to develop sentence fluency skills. As you play a piece of music, let students close their eyes and enjoy it. Then, play it a second time; only this time, invite them to pick a section and write a description of what they think is happening. Challenge students to capture the same fluidity of the music in their descriptions. From "Peter and the Wolf," one sixth-grade student wrote: "I could really tell when the scary part was coming. The music sped up and got faster and faster and I felt myself tensing up until BAM, the wolf pounced."

CRAFTING WELL-BUILT SENTENCES

Which Is Better?

Share two versions of a piece of writing. They will have the same content, but very different sounds. One should be made up of short, choppy sentences; for example:

> We went to the beach. It was sunny. It was warm. We had fun.
> We flew kites and ate hot dogs.

And the other, one continuous sentence:

> We spent a warm, sunny day at the beach eating hot dogs and flying kites.

Ask students which version they prefer and why. Discuss how the flow of the sentence can enhance meaning. You may have to share a number of examples before students begin to hear the differences.

Extra, Extra, Read All About It

Teach students the types of sentences they can use in their writing by exploring the newspaper. First, explain that reporters need to make sense of the information they receive. When they tell their readers what was said, they may restate the questions and even quote some of the answers. Reporters will use various kinds of sentences in their articles. Second, hand out sections of the newspaper to small groups and ask them to find examples of different sentence patterns: declarative (makes a statement of fact or argument), interrogative (asks a question), imperative (gives a direct command), or exclamatory (makes a more forceful statement than the declarative). Then ask students to circle an example of each kind of sentence from their section of the newspaper. Share examples with the class. Discuss which types of sentences they would use in their writing for a story, an essay, or a piece of persuasion.

VARYING SENTENCE PATTERNS

End With a Noun

One of the best tips a teacher ever shared with Ruth to make her sentences more powerful was to end them with a noun. As Ruth reads other texts and revises her own, she finds the passages she believes to be the strongest do exactly that—they end with a noun. It's perfectly correct to use verbs, pronouns, and adjectives, but nouns seem to pack the most punch. Not in all cases, of course, but it is advice worth considering when you struggle with just the right way to say something. Take a sentence, such as the first one below, and play around with it. Try ending it with different parts of speech and decide which is the most effectively written sentence.

> A rolling stone gathers no moss. (noun)
> If a stone rolls, hardly any moss will be gathered. (verb)
> If you are concerned about moss gathering on a stone, roll it. (pronoun)
> When trying to get rid of moss, roll the stone quickly. (adverb)
> If you roll the stone, the moss will become smooth. (adjective)

Pass It On

Give students a short beginning sentence—"The night was dark and stormy," for example. They'll then take the last word of the sentence and begin the next sentence with that word: "Stormy, that wasn't even the half of it." Keep going until the stories or essays are finished:

> "It hadn't been this windy and rainy in years, and I felt a little scared all alone. Alone in my grandparents house for the first time, my common sense told me I had nothing to be frightened of, but every time the wind rattled the windows, I jumped."

Don't let it go on too long because the writing tends to get silly. Linking words from sentence to sentence helps students stay with the topic and gives the piece an almost poetic quality.

BREAKING THE "RULES" TO CREATE FLUENCY

Sentences and Fragments Bee

This game helps students develop an ear for hearing the difference between sentences and fragments. It can be played at all grade levels and is especially helpful to English language learners.

Line up a group of students. Ask the student at the front of the line: "Is this a sentence or a fragment?" Then, give an example:

> My cousin Luke (fragment)
> Come inside, now. (sentence)
> Here is your umbrella. (sentence)
> Who didn't want (fragment)
> The ugly old witch (fragment)

To remain standing, the student must give the right answer. If he or she misses, the student sits down, and the game continues. The last student standing is the winner.

Reading Aloud to Yourself

Reading their drafts aloud is a trick professional writers use to determine if they're breaking the rules effectively. However, getting students to do that hasn't been easy for us. At best, we've gotten mumbles, speed reads, or no reading at all. Our students were just too self-conscious to allow themselves the agony and the ecstasy of hearing how their words flowed across the page. It wasn't until we put a homemade phone in their hands that they successfully read their pieces without the concern of being overheard by others.

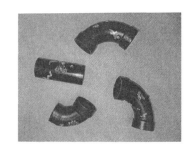

To make a simple "fluency phone" for your students, visit any home improvement store, go to the PVC plumbing pipe section, and describe what you need to a helpful salesperson: two to five short pieces of PVC pipe to fit together into the shape of a phone.

We decorate our fluency phones with stickers just to make them more fun, but the basic phone is simply a device, for students to read aloud and not feel conspicuous. And, as a bonus, when they read softly into the phone, not only can they hear every word and nuance, they can also hear the ocean.

Scoring Guides

Sample Papers

Lessons

Activities

FAQs

Conventions Activities

CHECKING SPELLING

Reading Backwards

To check for spelling errors, have students read their pieces backwards. That way, they focus on each word and don't get caught up in the meaning of the words in the sentence. Be sure they start with the last word and work all the way to the beginning. You won't believe how effective this is!

Those Nasty Homophones

Students seem to handle homophones (words that sound alike but are spelled differently) better when they're not taught in clusters. Some perennial problem words are: *their, there,* and *they're; to, too,* and *two; bare* and *bear; break* and *brake; deer* and *dear; I'll, aisle,* and *isle; pair, pear,* and *pare;* and *your* and *you're.* Teach one word at a time. For example, teach the word *pair,* a noun meaning two of a kind, and stop. When the student needs to spell the word *pare,* a verb meaning to trim down, teach them how to spell it and use it correctly.

PUNCTUATING EFFECTIVELY

Punctuation Walkabout

While editing for punctuation (periods, mainly), have students walk while reading one of their drafts. When they intend to insert a stop (a period), they must physically stop and stamp their feet. Expand to other punctuation marks by adding new motions, such as shooting a hand up in the air for an exclamation point or curling one arm around their head for a question mark. This kinesthetic approach helps students realize the importance of punctuation for indicating the end and tone of a thought.

Look Who's Talking

For students just learning to write dialogue, showing a change of speaker can be a big challenge. To teach them how to use quotation marks around spoken words, instruct students to highlight who is speaking in one color and what he or she is saying in another color. To get the students started, show them how to punctuate dialogue in one sentence and ask them to do the next. Remind them that every time there is a change of speaker, there should be a new paragraph.

CAPITALIZING CORRECTLY

Bouncing Ball

Give each student a super ball. (You may have to establish some ground rules for these—they have a way of flying out of control.) Call upon students to read a paragraph of their writing aloud to a partner. Every time there is a capital letter (or should be one), have them bounce their balls. If both students bounce balls at the same point, they should carry on. But if not, make sure the difference gets resolved so the capitals are in the right places. Switch roles so that both partners have their pieces edited for capitalization.

Context Capitals

Review the rules for using capitals in titles of books, magazines, headlines, and so forth. Your school reference collection may have an up-to-date style handbook, or perhaps your textbook contains the information. You can always check the Internet by searching "capital letters" or "capitals in titles."

Ask students to observe the way capitals are used on road signs, billboards, business signs, and other kinds of environmental text and find at least three examples of incorrect capitalization. Notice how businesses write their names or how slogans are capitalized. Discuss why a writer of signs might break the rule to create a look or feel.

APPLYING GRAMMAR AND USAGE

Pass It Back

Seat students in rows. The person at the front of each row writes a simple sentence (or takes one that you provide) and passes it back. The second person adds an appositive (a definition of someone or something), the third person adds internal punctuation.

- ❖ Charlie took his dog for a walk.

- ❖ Charlie my best friend since the third grade took his dog for a walk.

- ❖ Charlie, my best friend since the third grade, took his dog for a walk.

The rest of the row checks the sentence for corrections. From there, students rotate positions. This activity can be used to practice certain sentence parts, depending on what you ask students to add.

Use Literature

Read aloud Rick Walton's *Pig, Pigger, Piggest* (1997). Then have each student pick a word and add "er" and "est" to it. Illustrate by giving several examples, such as "cranky," "crankier," and "crankiest." You may wish to bring in objects such as stuffed animals to spur students' imagination: "teddy bear," "larger teddy bear," "largest teddy bear." This technique helps to teach comparative and superlative forms.

Concluding Thought

We hope the activities described in this chapter serve you and your students well. And to that end, we have one last piece of advice: Be fearless. The energy you bring to your work, your faith in your students, and your willingness to try new things right along with them will make all the difference. Commit to leaving no stone unturned in your quest to inspire young writers. Use these activities as starting points to stretch the bounds of your imagination. The writing lives of your young students are at stake.

Answers to the Questions Intermediate Teachers Ask Most

Teachers are inquisitive. We know because we are bombarded with good questions from them every day. Here are some of the most common ones about using the writing traits. Read through them for additional information on and clarification of points raised in this book. The answers will help you apply the traits to your teaching.

Are the traits a writing curriculum?

No. The traits have no scope and no sequence that unfold from year to year. We use the traits for assessment and as a shared vocabulary to describe what good writing looks like, whether the child is 5 or 15.

The traits should unfold as lessons and activities embedded in the writing curriculum. To be most effective, these lessons and activities should spring out of the grade-level curriculum and connect to important concepts found in literature, science, social studies, math, fine arts, and health (see Chapters 3 and 4 for examples). As you examine your curriculum with "trait eyes," you'll see the connections. Seize on them.

Use the traits to assess writing so you'll understand what students know and what they can do. Then focus your writing lessons and activities on improving their writing within the curriculum you're expected to teach. Use all the traits all the time. Forget any misguided notion that you should teach only a few traits to younger students or that you should assign different traits to different grades. Students in all grades need all traits every time they write. The traits bring the writing curriculum to life. But they are *not* the curriculum.

In what order should I cover the traits?

We start with the ideas trait because most writing begins with figuring out what to say and we end with conventions because most writing finishes with figuring out how it will look. However, there is no "right order" in between. You should cover the traits in the order that makes the most sense for your students and their needs. Once students have drafted a few pieces and you've assessed those papers using the scoring guides on pages 24–29, let their scores determine the sequence in which you cover the traits.

Isn't it punitive to give a score of 1?

A score of 1 is not a final summative evaluation. It's a message to the writer that he or she has work to do to show strength in the trait. It's an indicator of where the piece is right now and how much work it will need to become stronger in the trait, but nothing more. It's okay to give 1s as long as you give students the tools and support they need to move beyond them. Over time, as students get scores of 2, 3, and higher, they will notice and appreciate the improvement. And they will recognize you as an honest assessor. That's important.

Doesn't a score of 6 send a message that there's absolutely no room for improvement?

It's sometimes hard to give 6s out of fear that students will think their work is perfect and, thus, stop trying. It's important to remember that a 6 doesn't mean perfect. It means, "Good for you. You show control in the trait." That's it. There's always room for more. Challenge the student to write in a different mode, for instance, to stretch him or her as a writer.

How often should I use prompts to help students get started?

The best rule of thumb is fifty-fifty. About half the time students should write on topics of their own choosing, and about half the time they should be given relevant, stimulating, open-ended prompts.

How should I teach spelling?

There is no one way to teach spelling that will help every child. Like every other complex task, you need a variety of ways to approach it. For example, you may want to teach students how to use phonics and orthographic features (word parts) to help them spell. At the same time, be sure to let students know that there are some words that don't sound one bit like the way they are spelled, so they'll just have to learn them. Students should have lists of commonly spelled words at their desks or in their writing notebooks. Teach them how to use spell check on the computer. Finally, allow students to ask, "How do you spell . . . ?" so they don't get hung up on a word and lose track of what they're writing about. For more on teaching spelling, see page 102.

Why do parents worry so much about conventions?

Parents probably got feedback mostly on conventions during their school years, so it only makes sense that they are looking for the same emphasis on conventions from their children's teachers. However, if you teach conventions in the context of real writing (preferably the students' own writing), you need to explain that to parents. Parents will be supportive if they understand the plan. Explain to them that their child will receive focused and explicit help in conventions, but will be applying them to real writing, not to words and sentences in isolation. Also, explain that learning to apply conventions correctly takes time. Although their child may not be using commas and spelling words like *because* correctly, perhaps he or she is capitalizing the first letter of each sentence and spelling words like *from* correctly. This is cause for celebration. In time, the child will learn the more sophisticated matters.

PROFESSIONAL RESOURCES CITED

Culham, R. (2009). *Daily trait warm-ups: 180 revision and editing activities to kick off writing time.* New York: Scholastic.

Culham, R. & Coutu, R. (2009). *Getting started with the traits: K–2.* New York: Scholastic.

Fox, M. (1993). *Radical reflections: Passionate opinion on teaching, learning, and living.* New York: Harcourt.

King, S. (2000). *On writing: A memoir of the craft.* New York: Scribner.

CHILDREN'S LITERATURE CITED

Abercrombie, B. (1995). *Charlie Anderson.* New York: Simon & Schuster.

Avi. (1999). *Midnight magic.* New York: Scholastic.

Babbitt, N. (1975). *Tuck everlasting.* New York: Farrar, Straus.

Banks, L. R. (1980). *The Indian in the cupboard.* New York: Avon.

Bloom, B. (1999). *Wolf!* New York: Orchard.

Capote, T. (1956). *A Christmas memory.* New York: Random House.

Christelow, E. (1995). *What do authors do?* New York: Clarion.

Cisneros, S. (1991). *Woman hollering creek.* New York: Random House.

Cobb, V. (1997). *Blood & gore like you've never seen!* New York: Scholastic.

Creech, S. (1994). *Walk two moons.* New York: HarperCollins.

Curtis, C. P. (1999). *Bud, not Buddy.* New York: Delacorte.

Dahl, R. (1961). *James and the giant peach.* New York: Alfred A. Knopf.

Dahl, R. (1988). *Matilda.* New York: Viking.

Davies, N. (2001). *One tiny turtle.* Cambridge, MA: Candlewick.

Duke, K. (1992). *Aunt Isabel tells a good one.* New York: Dutton.

Fletcher, R. (1997). *Spider boy.* New York: Clarion.

Fox, M. (1989). *Koala Lou.* New York: Harcourt.

Fox, M. (1994). *Tough Boris.* New York: Harcourt.

Frame, J. A. (2003). *Yesterday I had the blues.* Berkeley, CA: Tricycle.

Fritz, J. (1982). *Homesick: My own story.* New York: Bantam Doubleday Dell.

Hesse, K. (1999). *Come on, rain!* New York: Scholastic.

Lester, H. (1997). *Author: A true story.* New York: Houghton Mifflin.

Liao, J. (2006). *The sound of color: A journey of the imagination.* Boston: Little, Brown.

Moss, M. (2006). *Amelia's Notebook.* New York: Simon & Schuster.

Muth, J. J. (2002). *The three questions.* New York: Scholastic.

Nobisso, J. (2004). *Show, don't tell! Secrets of writing.* Westhampton Beach, NY: Gingerbread House.

O'Connor, J. (2006). *Fancy Nancy.* New York: HarperCollins.

O'Neill, M. (1961). *Hailstones and halibut bones.* Garden City, NY: Doubleday.

Reynolds, P. H. (2004). *Ish.* Cambridge, MA: Candlewick.

Rose, D. L. (2001). *Into the a, b, sea.* New York: Scholastic.

Rowling, J. K. (1997). *Harry Potter and the sorcerer's stone.* New York: Scholastic.

Sachar, L. (1998). *Holes.* New York: Farrar, Straus.

Schotter, R. (2006). *The boy who loved words.* New York: Schwartz & Wade.

Schotter, R. (1997). *Nothing ever happens on 90th Street.* New York: Orchard Books.

Teague, M. (1996). *The secret shortcut.* New York: Scholastic.

Walton, R. (1997). *Pig, pigger, piggest.* Layton, UT: Gibbs Smith.

Watt, M. (2006). *Scaredy Squirrel.* Toronto, ON: Kids Can Press.

Watt, M. (2007). *Scaredy Squirrel makes a friend.* Toronto, ON: Kids Can Press.

White, E. B. (1952). *Charlotte's web.* New York: HarperCollins.

Wisniewski, D. (1998). *The secret knowledge of grown-ups.* New York: William Morrow.

Wong, J. S. (2002). *You have to write.* New York: Margaret K. McElderry.

Revision Checklist

I've revised for:

☐ **Ideas:** I've selected one topic, focused it, and used specific details to describe it.

☐ **Organization:** I've written an attention-grabbing lead, organized my details in a logical way, and wrapped it all up in the conclusion.

☐ **Voice:** I've written in a way that sets the right tone for my piece, targets my audience, and sounds fresh and original.

☐ **Word Choice:** I've used strong verbs and other specific and accurate words that add sparkle to my writing.

☐ **Sentence Fluency:** I've used sentences with different lengths and patterns to add rhythm to my writing, and I've taken some risks and tried some new ways to write sentences.

☐ **Conventions:** I've checked my spelling, capitalization, punctuation, and grammar and usage for accuracy. My use of conventions will help to guide the reader through the text.

Traits in my writing that still need attention and my plan for improving them:

☐ Ideas: _____   ☐ Word Choice: _____

_____   _____

☐ Organization: _____   ☐ Sentence Fluency: _____

_____   _____

☐ Voice: _____   ☐ Conventions: _____

_____   _____

Getting Started With the Traits: Grades 3–5 © 2009 Ruth Culham and Raymond Coutu, Scholastic.

Editor's Marks

for Beginning Writers

ℰ	Delete material.	The writing is is good.
(sp)	Correct the spelling or spell it out.	We are learning ②traits this week.
⌒	Close space.	To day is publishing day.
∧	Insert a letter, word, or phrase.	My teacher has books. wonderful
∧	Change a letter.	She is a great wroter.
#	Add a space.	Don't forget agood introduction.
∿	Transpose letters or words.	She raed the piece with flair!
≡	Change to a capital letter.	We have j.k. Rowling to thank for Harry Potter's magic.
/	Change to a lowercase letter.	The "Proof is in the Pudding" was his favorite saying.
¶	Start a new paragraph.	"What day is it?" he inquired. "It's Christmas," returned Tiny Tim.
⊙	Add a period.	Use all the traits as you write ⊙

Student-Friendly Scoring Guide
Organization

I've Got It!

❋ I included a bold beginning.

❋ I've shown how the ideas connect.

❋ My ideas are in an order that really works.

❋ My ending leaves you with something to think about.

On My Way

❋ There is a beginning, but it's not particularly special.

❋ Most of my details fit logically; I could move or get rid of others.

❋ Sections of my writing flow logically, but other parts seem out of place.

❋ My ending is not original, but it does clearly show where the piece stops.

Just Starting

❋ I forgot to write a clear introduction to this piece.

❋ I have the right "stuff" to work with, but it's not in order.

❋ The order of my details are jumbled and confusing.

❋ Oops! I forgot to end my piece with a wrap-up.

Student-Friendly Scoring Guide
Ideas

I've Got It!

❋ I picked a topic and stuck with it.

❋ My topic is small enough to handle.

❋ I know a lot about this topic.

❋ My topic is bursting with fascinating details.

On My Way

❋ I've wandered off my main topic in a few places.

❋ My topic might be a little too big to handle.

❋ I know enough about my topic to get started.

❋ Some of my details are too general.

Just Starting

❋ I have included several ideas that might make a good topic.

❋ No one idea stands out as most important.

❋ I'm still looking for a topic that will work well.

❋ My details are fuzzy or not clear.

Getting Started With the Traits: Grades 3–5 © 2009 Ruth Culham and Raymond Coutu, Scholastic.

Student-Friendly Scoring Guide
Word Choice

I've Got It!

❋ I used strong verbs to add energy.

❋ My words are specific and are colorful, fresh, and snappy.

❋ My words help my reader see my ideas.

❋ My words are accurate and used correctly.

On My Way

❋ Only one or two verbs stand out in this piece.

❋ I've used many ordinary words; there's no sparkle.

❋ My words give the reader the most general picture of the idea.

❋ I've misused some words or overused others.

Just Starting

❋ I haven't used any verbs that convey energy.

❋ I've left out key words.

❋ Many of my words are repetitive or just wrong.

❋ I'm confused about how to use words as I write.

Student-Friendly Scoring Guide
Voice

I've Got It!

❋ I used a distinctive tone that works with the topic.

❋ I was clear about why I was writing, so my voice is believable.

❋ The audience will connect with what I wrote.

❋ I tried some new ways of expressing myself to add interest.

On My Way

❋ I played it safe. You only get a glimpse of me in this piece.

❋ I wasn't always clear about my purpose, so my voice fades in and out.

❋ I'm only mildly interested in this topic.

❋ I didn't try to express myself in new ways.

Just Starting

❋ I didn't share anything about what I think and feel in this piece.

❋ I'm not sure what or why I'm writing.

❋ This topic is not interesting to me at all.

❋ I'm bored and it shows.

Student-Friendly Scoring Guide
Conventions

I've Got It!

* My spelling is magnificent.
* I put capital letters in all the right places.
* I used punctuation correctly to make my writing easy to read.
* I used correct grammar and indented paragraphs where necessary.

On My Way

* Only my simpler words are spelled correctly.
* I used capital letters in easy spots.
* I have correct punctuation in some places but not in others.
* There are a few places where the grammar isn't quite right, and I've forgotten to indicate paragraphs except at the beginning.

Just Starting

* My words are hard to read and understand because of the spelling.
* I've not followed the rules for capitalization.
* My punctuation is missing or in the wrong places.
* The grammar needs a lot of work. I forgot about using paragraphs.

Student-Friendly Scoring Guide
Sentence Fluency

I've Got It!

* My sentences are well-built and have varied beginnings.
* I've tried to write using interjections or fragments to create variety.
* My sentences read smoothly.
* I've varied the length and structure of my sentences.

On My Way

* My sentences are working pretty well.
* I've tried a couple of ways to begin my sentences differently, but could do more.
* When I read my piece aloud, there are a few places that need smoothing.
* I might put some sentences together or I could cut a few in two.

Just Starting

* My sentences aren't working well.
* The beginnings of my sentences sound the same.
* I'm having trouble reading my piece aloud.
* I've used words like "and" or "but" too many times.

Getting Started With the Traits: Grades 3–5 © 2009 Ruth Culham and Raymond Coutu, Scholastic.